# QUASI-JUDICIAL HANDBOOK:
## A GUIDE FOR BOARDS MAKING DEVELOPMENT REGULATION DECISIONS

2017

UNC
SCHOOL OF GOVERNMENT

The School of Government at the University of North Carolina at Chapel Hill works to improve the lives of North Carolinians by engaging in practical scholarship that helps public officials and citizens understand and improve state and local government. Established in 1931 as the Institute of Government, the School provides educational, advisory, and research services for state and local governments. The School of Government is also home to a nationally ranked Master of Public Administration program, the North Carolina Judicial College, and specialized centers focused on community and economic development, information technology, and environmental finance.

As the largest university-based local government training, advisory, and research organization in the United States, the School of Government offers up to 200 courses, webinars, and specialized conferences for more than 12,000 public officials each year. In addition, faculty members annually publish approximately 50 books, manuals, reports, articles, bulletins, and other print and online content related to state and local government. The School also produces the *Daily Bulletin Online* each day the General Assembly is in session, reporting on activities for members of the legislature and others who need to follow the course of legislation.

Operating support for the School of Government's programs and activities comes from many sources, including state appropriations, local government membership dues, private contributions, publication sales, course fees, and service contracts.

Visit sog.unc.edu or call 919.966.5381 for more information on the School's courses, publications, programs, and services.

Michael R. Smith, DEAN
Thomas H. Thornburg, SENIOR ASSOCIATE DEAN
Frayda S. Bluestein, ASSOCIATE DEAN FOR FACULTY DEVELOPMENT
Johnny Burleson, ASSOCIATE DEAN FOR DEVELOPMENT
Michael Vollmer, ASSOCIATE DEAN FOR ADMINISTRATION
Linda H. Weiner, ASSOCIATE DEAN FOR OPERATIONS
Janet Holston, DIRECTOR OF STRATEGY AND INNOVATION

FACULTY

| | | |
|---|---|---|
| Whitney Afonso | Norma Houston | Kimberly L. Nelson |
| Trey Allen | Cheryl Daniels Howell | David W. Owens |
| Gregory S. Allison | Jeffrey A. Hughes | LaToya B. Powell |
| David N. Ammons | Willow S. Jacobson | William C. Rivenbark |
| Ann M. Anderson | Robert P. Joyce | Dale J. Roenigk |
| Maureen Berner | Diane M. Juffras | John Rubin |
| Mark F. Botts | Dona G. Lewandowski | Jessica Smith |
| Anita R. Brown-Graham | Adam Lovelady | Meredith Smith |
| Peg Carlson | James M. Markham | Carl W. Stenberg III |
| Leisha DeHart-Davis | Christopher B. McLaughlin | John B. Stephens |
| Shea Riggsbee Denning | Kara A. Millonzi | Charles Szypszak |
| Sara DePasquale | Jill D. Moore | Shannon H. Tufts |
| James C. Drennan | Jonathan Q. Morgan | Aimee N. Wall |
| Richard D. Ducker | Ricardo S. Morse | Jeffrey B. Welty |
| Robert L. Farb | C. Tyler Mulligan | Richard B. Whisnant |

# Contents

# Acknowledgments

This book has benefited greatly from the comments of experienced practitioners who generously agreed to review it. Attorney T. J. Morphis (Chapel Hill) organized a review by members of the Zoning, Planning, and Land Use Law Section of the North Carolina Bar Association. These attorneys have considerable experience handling quasi-judicial matters, representing local governments, applicants, and neighbors before city and county boards. Attorneys contributing comments include Al Benshoff (Concord), James Bryan (Hillsborough), Anne Fisher (Blowing Rock), Lisa Glover (Cary), Ralph Karpinos (Chapel Hill), and Robert Oast (Asheville). Ramona Bartos of the State Historic Preservation Office kindly reviewed the chapter on certificates of appropriateness. The many helpful comments of these reviewers are gratefully acknowledged.

For decades the standard handbook for boards handling variances, special use permits, and appeals in this state was *The Zoning Board of Adjustment in North Carolina*. This book builds on that foundation, and we owe its authors, Mike Brough and Phil Green, our gratitude and appreciation as well. We also thank our colleague Rich Ducker, whose decades of training for boards of adjustment are reflected in our work and in this publication.

David W. Owens
Adam S. Lovelady
Chapel Hill
May 2017

# Chapter 1
# **Introduction**

## **Nature of Quasi-Judicial Decisions**

As its name suggests, a *quasi-judicial* decision is similar to a *court* decision in several ways. For one, as with a court proceeding, a quasi-judicial proceeding requires the deciding board to adjudicate how the general law applies to a particular situation. For another, a quasi-judicial adjudication is based on evidence and standards—thus requiring the board to use its judgment in drawing its conclusion. Also, as with a court case, the board must follow rules in order to protect the constitutional due process rights of the parties. These similarities are discussed in greater detail below.

**General law applied to a particular situation.** Land use ordinances outline standards for certain types of developments and for making decisions regarding them. The quasi-judicial hearing is the process by which those standards are applied to specific properties. So, for example, a land use ordinance provides a way for a property owner to be granted a variance from the zoning rules if those rules create an "unnecessary hardship." At an evidentiary hearing, a local board would try to apply that general rule to a particular piece of property by examining the evidence in that particular case and asking: Does the ordinance create an unnecessary hardship for *this* property?

**Judgment.** Quasi-judicial decisions require the board to take in evidence and use its judgment to make factual as well as legal determinations about whether a particular property or project meets the standards established by the land use ordinance. Such standards include the variance standard of unnecessary hardship, as noted above, as well as the special use permit standard of being in harmony with the area. Quasi-judicial hearings also adjudicate appeals of staff decisions, certificates of appropriateness (historic preservation), and similar land use standards.

**Constitutional due process rights.** Because the board is adjudicating property rights, it must adhere to specific rules to ensure the constitutional due process rights of the parties. The ordinance must provide clear guidance on standards the applicant must meet. Parties must be provided proper notice of the land use standards that apply and of the hearing itself. At the hearing, the parties have the rights to present evidence, cross-examine witnesses, and provide rebuttal. Board members must be impartial decision-makers. In addition, the parties have a right to appeal the board's decision.

## Decisions Subject to Quasi-Judicial Procedures

As has been noted, a board follows quasi-judicial procedures when it takes in evidence and applies its judgment in making certain land use decisions. The accompanying chart outlines common land use decisions that require quasi-judicial adjudication. In addition to the decision types listed in the chart, other land use decisions that involve subjective standards also require quasi-judicial procedures. For example, a local development regulation may include subjective standards for subdivision plat or site plan approvals. If that is the case, decisions on those applications also must follow quasi-judicial procedures.

The quasi-judicial process is just one type of land use decision. Alternatively, land use decisions may be administrative or legislative. Administrative decisions—such as basic zoning permits—are based on objective criteria in the ordinance and typically are made by zoning staff. These decisions tend to be made fairly quickly and with greater predictability but provide little room for the consideration of special circumstances and conditions. Legislative decisions—such as rezonings and conditional zoning— are made at the discretion of the governing board. These decisions require much more public input and discretion, which can slow down the process and make it less predictable.

## Boards That Make Quasi-Judicial Decisions

North Carolina law allows some flexibility as to which boards handle which decisions, but those assignments must be set out in the applicable land use ordinance. The board of adjustment may be assigned to handle specific

## Common Quasi-Judicial Decision Types and the Standards That Apply to Them

| Decision Type | Standard |
| --- | --- |
| Variance | Has the applicant shown that |
| | An unnecessary hardship would result from the strict application of the ordinance? |
| | The hardship results from conditions peculiar to the property, such as location, size, or topography? |
| | The hardship did not result from actions taken by the applicant or the property owner? |
| | The requested variance is consistent with the spirit, purpose, and intent of the ordinance such that public safety is secured and substantial justice is achieved? |
| | (statutory standard) |
| Special and conditional use permits | Is the project |
| | In harmony with the area? |
| | Consistent with applicable plans? |
| | Not harmful to health and public safety? |
| | Not harmful to neighboring property values? |
| | (standards are specific to the local ordinance but commonly include the above) |
| Appeal of staff decisions | Based on the evidence and law, did staff make the correct decision? |
| Certificates of Appropriateness (historic preservation) | Is the project incongruous with the special character of the district or landmark? |
| | (as identified in adopted design standards and guidelines) |

quasi-judicial decisions, among them, zoning variances and appeals of staff decisions. Other boards also are authorized to handle quasi-judicial matters, including the governing board, the planning board, and the historic preservation commission. Special use permits may be assigned to the board of adjustment, governing board, or planning board. Any or all of the duties of the board of adjustment may be assigned to the planning board or the governing board. In addition, the duties of the preservation commission may be assigned to the planning board.

Whether a decision is quasi-judicial is based on the type of standard to be applied, not the board making the decision. So, at one meeting a planning board could hold an evidentiary hearing on a special use permit (a quasi-judicial matter) and then make an advisory decision on an amendment to the zoning ordinance (a legislative matter).

Similarly, at a single meeting the governing board could take a ministerial action (on a final subdivision plat, for example), take a quasi-judicial action (on a special use permit), and take a legislative action (to amend the zoning ordinance). There are significant procedural differences between these types of decisions, including different rules on conflicts of interest, communication with the public, community input, and discretion in decision-making. In general, it is advisable for the governing board to focus on legislative actions and to allow local government staff to handle ministerial actions and other local boards to handle quasi-judicial matters.

## Role of the Board and Others

The board is the decision-maker. Board members must review the evidence in the record, critically evaluate the credibility of witnesses and weight of the evidence, determine contested facts, and apply those facts to the standards to reach a decision. Through this process the board must adhere to certain rules of procedure.

Local government staff coordinates the process. They accept and review applications, coordinate and provide analysis, collect and manage the record of evidence, and assist the board with review and action.

Certain individuals with a special interest in the outcome have standing to act as parties in the case. This includes the applicant and property owner and may also include neighbors who would suffer special damages from the outcome of the case. Other individuals may participate as witnesses but do not enjoy the rights of parties with standing.

These roles and responsibilities are discussed in greater detail throughout this handbook.

## About This Book

This handbook is designed as a practical resource for North Carolina local government boards in making quasi-judicial land use decisions. Such bodies include the governing board, the board of adjustment, the planning board, the preservation commission, and/or other boards, depending on the assignment of decision-making authority for the particular jurisdiction.

The handbook is organized into ten chapters covering a range of quasi-judicial procedures and types of decisions. Following this introduction, Chapter 2 outlines the organization and responsibilities of boards of adjustment. This is followed by the set of chapters 3 through 5, which outline the steps in reaching a quasi-judicial decision. Chapter 3 explores the rules and procedures to be followed before an evidentiary hearing takes place, such as providing proper notice, preparing the preliminary record (application, staff analysis, and other documents), and establishing the rules of impartiality. Chapter 4 outlines the steps of conducting an evidentiary hearing, presenting a combination of practical tips and a discussion of the constitutionally required elements of due process. Chapter 5 provides guidance on the procedures involved in making a quasi-judicial decision, including the burden of providing sufficient evidence, findings of fact, consideration of conditions, voting, and the decision document.

Chapters 6 through 9 provide greater detail on four types of quasi-judicial decisions, as follows:

- variances (Chapter 6),
- special use permits (Chapter 7),
- certificates of appropriateness (Chapter 8), and
- appeals of staff decisions (Chapter 9).

Finally, Chapter 10 explores the process for appealing quasi-judicial decisions to superior court.

The North Carolina General Statutes (hereinafter G.S.) have, since 1923, authorized and defined the role of boards of adjustment. As in many other states, legislation authorizing N.C. local governments to undertake zoning was based on the Standard State Zoning Enabling Act recommended by the U.S. Department of Commerce in 1922. Although many states share this common starting point, state statutes have evolved independently over the ensuing decades, so some caution is warranted in applying the legal experience gained in other states.

Given the nature of quasi-judicial decisions, many legal topics are covered here. Select citations for statutes and cases are included for reference and convenience. Additional resources are available for more in-depth discussion of legal topics, including David Owens's *Land Use Law in North Carolina* (2nd ed., 2011); Adam Lovelady's *Land Subdivision Regulation in North Carolina* (2015); and posts by David and Adam on *Coates' Canons: NC Local Government Law* blog (http://canons.sog.unc.edu). For information about training on topics of land use law, check out the Planning and Development Regulation microsite on the School of Government website (www.sog.unc.edu/organizations/planning).

# Chapter 2
# Organization of the Board of Adjustment

In most North Carolina cities and counties, the zoning and development regulation ordinances create a board of adjustment to make quasi-judicial decisions. Given the key role the board of adjustment plays in quasi-judicial decision-making, this chapter reviews the legal requirements regarding its composition and organization.

## Authority and Duties

State law generally assumes that local development regulations will create a board of adjustment and assign it the duties of hearing variance petitions and appeals of staff determinations (such as appealing a notice of violation or the staff's interpretation of the ordinance). The law also allows the board of adjustment to handle final decision-making on special and conditional use permits.

It is important to note, however, that North Carolina law gives cities and counties flexibility on this point. According to the General Statutes, local ordinances "may provide for" a board of adjustment.[1] Most local ordinances do just that. But the statute does not mandate creation of a board of adjustment. The courts have confirmed that having a board of adjustment is not mandatory.[2] If no board of adjustment is created, however, that leaves the question of how the functions normally assigned to the board will be carried out.

The General Statutes provide an important option for addressing this question. Any of the functions of a board of adjustment may be assigned to

---

1. Section 160A-388(a) of the North Carolina General Statutes (hereinafter G.S.). The county statute on boards of adjustment, G.S. 153A-345, was repealed in 2013 and replaced with G.S. 153A-345.1, which makes G.S. 160A-388 applicable to counties.
2. Bd. of Adjustment v. Town of Swansboro, 334 N.C. 421, 432 S.E. 2d 310 (1993).

the planning board or to the governing board.[3] In jurisdictions with small populations and little growth, the workload of the board of adjustment may be so modest that creating a separate board to hear only a few cases is not warranted. In such instances, it is fairly common to assign all of the functions of both the planning board and the board of adjustment to a single joint board. A very few local governments assign the functions of the board of adjustment to the governing board, but of those that do, they typically review only a single variance petition every few years.

It is also possible for multiple jurisdictions to have a joint board of adjustment, and several cities and counties have created joint planning programs. In these instances, each local government can establish its own board of adjustment to hear cases arising within its jurisdiction, but the General Statutes also allow local governments to create a single joint board to hear cases arising within any of the included jurisdictions.[4]

## Appointments

State law does not mandate how appointments to the board of adjustment are made. It is thus permissible for the ordinance to assign the responsibility for making appointments to the mayor or chair of the board of county commissioners or even to the city or county manager. The practical reality, though, is that in virtually all instances North Carolina ordinances authorize a jurisdiction's governing board to make appointments to the board of adjustment.

It is fairly common for the local ordinance or rules of procedure to specify a process for how the board is to make these appointments. For example, the governing board will often ask interested persons to apply for a seat on the board, specify what information applicants will need to provide, and may require that a public meeting or hearing be held where the board can interview or hear from applicants. The board then makes the appointments by majority vote.

The General Statutes do not require that an appointee be a resident of the jurisdiction but allow local governments to include that as a require-

---

3. G.S. 160A-388(a).
4. G.S. 160A-461.

ment if so desired.[5] It is permissible, but not common, for the ordinance to specify other qualifications for appointment, such as allocating seats for geographic diversity.

One exception to this general flexibility on the residency issue arises when a county zones less than the entire county. In such situations, each area within the county that is zoned is, if practical, to have at least one resident appointed to the county board of adjustment. Another exception to the same rule involves extraterritorial members, which is discussed below.

## Size

The number of members on a board of adjustment is another variable where the General Statutes allow some, but not unlimited, discretion. A board of adjustment must have at least five members.[6] The board can have more members but not fewer. The ordinance creating the board must specify the number of board members and the number of alternate members.

## Extraterritorial Members

A city that has extraterritorial jurisdiction (ETJ) for planning and development regulation must appoint extraterritorial members to its planning board and to the board of adjustment. This is not optional. The General Statutes require that these appointments be made.[7]

The number of extraterritorial members to be appointed is determined by the population of the extraterritorial area. Proportional representation is required,[8] meaning that each ETJ member should represent about the same number of residents as a member from inside the city. There must always be at least one extraterritorial member, with additional ETJ members to be appointed only after the estimated population of the ETJ area reaches the number of city residents represented by a single board member.

---

5. G.S. 153A-25; G.S. 160A-60.
6. G.S. 160A-388(a).
7. G.S. 160A-362.
8. *Id.*

## CALCULATION OF NUMBER OF ETJ MEMBERS NEEDED

Consider a city with a population of 10,000 persons and a five-member board of adjustment. That is one board of adjustment member for every 2,000 city residents. If this city has extraterritorial jurisdiction (ETJ) for planning, it must add additional members to the board of adjustment by appointing one ETJ member to the board of adjustment for every 2,000 ETJ residents. So if the estimated population of the ETJ area is 4,000 persons, the city would have to appoint two ETJ members to serve alongside the five members from within the city, producing a board of adjustment of seven total members (five "inside" members and two ETJ members).

What if there were 5,000 residents in the ETJ area? The city would still only have to appoint two ETJ members, as the statutes say that an additional member is required only when the calculation produces the need for a full fraction. In essence, the city rounds down, so if the calculation is that it needs 2.5 members in this situation, only two appointments are required.

If the city wanted to keep the total board membership at five members, it could do so by allowing both "inside" and ETJ members to vote on all cases. But the makeup of the five-member board would still have to be proportional based on the respective populations within the corporate limits and in the ETJ. In the first example above, this would result in having four inside members and one ETJ member. The calculation is that with a population of 10,000, each of the four members would represent 2,500 citizens inside the city, so there would need to be one ETJ member for each 2,500 ETJ residents. While in this example there are less than 2,500 ETJ residents, the law requires at least one ETJ member, so the city would need to have four inside members and one ETJ member. Given the complexity of this calculation, most cities find it easier to have a set number of inside members and then add ETJ members as needed.

The General Statutes also provide that the extraterritorial members of city boards of adjustment are to be appointed by the county board of commissioners rather than by the city.[9] If the extraterritorial area is in more than one county, each county appoints members for the area within their respective county. Although the statutes do not specify this, presumably the number of appointees made by each county is to be based on the population of the extraterritorial area within that county. However, if the county board of commissioners fails to appoint ETJ members within ninety days

---

9. *Id.*

of receiving a resolution from the city requesting that the appointments be made, the city governing board is then authorized to make them.

The General Statutes also specify the process a county must follow in appointing new extraterritorial members as a result of a city extending its extraterritorial jurisdiction. In such situations, the county must hold a public hearing on the appointments. Notice of the hearing is to be published in the newspaper once a week for two successive weeks.[10] The county commissioners may pick only from among those persons who applied to be on the board at or before this hearing.

Finally, the General Statues specify that the extraterritorial members should be residents of the extraterritorial area. If an insufficient number of area residents are willing to be appointed, the county commissioners may appoint other county residents to fill the needed number of seats. The statute does not require that these appointees reside outside the city, only that they be residents of the county.

The city ordinance determines the matters on which the extraterritorial members are allowed to vote. If authorized by the ordinance, ETJ members are allowed to vote on any and all matters coming before the board. If the city ordinance does not so specify, ETJ members may vote only on matters arising within the extraterritorial area.

## Alternate Members

The General Statutes allow but do not require boards of adjustment to have alternate members.[11] This is a common and worthwhile practice, however. If the ordinance provides for alternate members, they must be appointed for the same terms, at the same time, and in the same manner as regular members.

Alternate members participate and vote on matters when a regular member of the board is not available. It may be that a member is simply unable to attend a particular meeting. It also could be that a regular member is present but has a conflict of interest on an individual case and therefore is not allowed to participate in the matter. Or, there may be a vacant seat

---

10. *Id.*
11. G.S. 160A-388(a).

on the board. In any of these circumstances, an alternate member allows the board to proceed and conduct its business with a full complement of voting members.

Having an alternate member available is particularly important when hearing requests for variances. State law requires a four-fifths majority of the board to grant a variance. Thus, a five-member board with one person absent and no alternate would be unable to achieve a four-fifths majority for granting a variance without a unanimous vote; a 3 to 1 vote would be insufficient. While the voting calculation is slightly different, the same practical problem arises when a member has a conflict of interest. That member's seat is not counted in the calculation, but the four-fifths requirement still applies. So, in the event that one member of a five-member board has a conflict of interest, the applicant must get four-fifths of the four members who are eligible to vote. In that case, a 3 to 1 vote in favor is only three-quarters of the four voters, not the required four-fifths. Having an alternate member would restore the board to having five votes in either circumstance, meaning that a unanimous vote would not be necessary to grant a variance. In situations where a unanimous vote would be necessary, many boards give the petitioner the choice of continuing the hearing to a later date or proceeding with only four voting members.

In addition, the use of alternates allows meetings, hearings, and decisions to proceed in an orderly, predictable, and efficient fashion. Regular members must be absent sometimes, or at times have unavoidable conflicts, so having no alternate member available can lead to meetings being canceled or delayed. For these reasons, most ordinances provide for alternate members for boards of adjustment.

Some boards have their alternate members attend all meetings, while others call them in only if it is clear that their participation will be needed. Either practice is legally acceptable, but regular attendance by alternates can be helpful for several reasons. First, it gives alternate members exposure to the work of the board, thereby helping them be more prepared to act when needed. Second, the need for an alternate is sometimes not known until the meeting itself. A regular member may have to miss the meeting at the last minute. Or it may be at the hearing that a member discovers a conflict of interest. Having an alternate member present and ready to participate is useful in those situations.

An alternate member can be called into service for an entire meeting or for a single case. If serving for a regular member who is absent, the alternate will fully participate in all matters arising at that meeting. Conversely, if a regular member is present but has a conflict of interest on one of several cases coming before the board, the alternate will serve for only the one case involving that conflict, with the regular member resuming his or her seat for the other cases. While serving for a regular member, the alternate member has the same powers and duties as the regular member. It is perfectly acceptable for an alternate member to observe the proceedings, but active participation by an alternate who is not acting on a given case raises due process problems that are best avoided by having the alternate observe only.

Provisions for appointing alternate members from inside both the city and the extraterritorial jurisdiction, though not addressed by state statute, are provided in many city ordinances. Such ordinances commonly specify that alternates from inside the city limits may serve only to replace regular members from inside the city and that ETJ alternates may serve only to replace ETJ regular members. Given that the role of city/ETJ alternates is not specified by statute, it is prudent to have city ordinances include instructions on the matter.

## Term of Office

The General Statutes require that board of adjustment members be appointed to three-year terms of office.[12] Members may be reappointed, but each individual term must be for three years. An ordinance may limit the number of consecutive terms an individual may serve, but if there are no such limits in the ordinance, reappointment is solely at the discretion of the appointing board. While not specifically addressed by statute, the three-year term provision likely applies to alternate members as well, and that is the standard practice.

This is different from other local boards, on which members may serve at the pleasure of the appointing body. Use of a fixed term was an early feature of zoning law around the country, as it provides a degree of insulation from

---

12. *Id.*

political pressure for board of adjustment members. They are appointed to fairly apply the ordinances as they are written, acting in a judicious capacity. Like judges, they are not to be swayed by popular opinion or political pressure. Having a fixed, set term of office is intended to help secure just that.

Members can be removed from office during their term only for good cause. In this context, "cause" includes intentional failure to discharge one's duties, criminal misconduct in office, incapacity, and similar substantive problems. For example, the ordinance or rules of procedure may require regular attendance of board members and declare a seat vacated if the member misses too many meetings. Failure to faithfully execute one's duties by regularly missing meetings is cause for removal. Making an unpopular decision, or one not favored by the governing board, is not.

Staggered terms are expressly allowed when a board is first created and when existing terms expire.[13] In such cases, some members are appointed to one-year terms, some to two-year terms, and some to three-year terms. This provides continuity going forward, as one or two seats become open each year for reappointment or appointment of new members and avoids all member terms expiring at the same time. While this practice is not required by state law, it is certainly advisable.

## Oath of Office

Both the North Carolina Constitution and the General Statutes require those appointed to public office to take an oath of office.[14] The statutes do not explicitly state that a position on the board of adjustment is a public office, but it likely is, so members would be well advised to take an oath of office when first seated on the board.

The state constitution provides the form of the oath, as follows:

I, _____, do solemnly swear (or affirm) that I will support and maintain the Constitution and laws of the United States, and the Constitution and laws of North Carolina not inconsistent therewith, and that I will faithfully discharge the duties of my office as [a member of the board of adjustment], so help me God.

13. *Id.*
14. N.C. CONST. art. VI, § 7; G.S. 153A-26; G.S. 160A-61.

A person with conscientious objection may affirm rather than swear and may omit the phrase "so help me God."[15]

The oath of office may be administered by the mayor or the chair of the board of county commissioners, the city or county clerk, or any notary public.[16] The oath is usually administered to all new members at the beginning of the first meeting of their term of office. It also may be administered prior to the meeting. The oath of office is signed and filed with the city or county clerk.

## Dual Office Holding

The state constitution and statutes prohibit a person from holding more than two elected or appointed offices.[17] This means that a person appointed to a board of adjustment may serve in only one other elected or appointed office. A person who violates this requirement forfeits the office.

There is one important qualification to this restriction that can come into play with boards of adjustment. If a statute or ordinance provides that appointment to one office automatically makes the appointee a member of a second board (often as an ex officio member), that is not considered dual office holding. For example, a small town could, through its ordinance, provide that all members of the planning board automatically serve as the board of adjustment. This would not be considered a second office for these members since they automatically are appointed to the second board (the board of adjustment) as a result of being appointed to the first board (the planning board). A simpler way to accomplish the same thing would be to create only one board in the ordinance and assign all of the functions of a planning board and a board of adjustment to that single board. In either instance, the members are considered to hold one rather than two offices, thus not triggering the dual office holding prohibition.

---

15. G.S. 11-4. The same is true for an oath to tell the truth that is administered to witnesses at evidentiary hearings.

16. G.S. 11-7.1. The oath may also be administered by a judge, magistrate, clerk of court, register of deeds, or member of the General Assembly.

17. N.C. CONST. art VI, § 9; G.S. 128-1 to -2.

## Officers

The General Statutes assume that a member will be appointed to chair the board of adjustment, but how the chair is selected and whether there are to be other officers are left to each local government to determine. The ordinance creating the board of adjustment or the board's rules of procedure specify how the chair is selected. The most common options are for the appointing board to designate a member as chair or for the board of adjustment to elect one of its members as chair. It is also common to have a vice-chair who can act as chair in the chair's absence or non-participation. It is also a good idea to specifically allow board members to select an interim chair to serve in those cases or meetings where neither the chair nor the vice-chair is available.

Typically city or county staff serve as clerk and secretary for the board of adjustment, keeping minutes, records, and other administrative duties. In the rare event that staff support is not provided, the board would need to designate one of its members to assure that this essential supporting work is done.

The General Statutes give the chair a few specific powers and duties.[18] For one, the chair is authorized to administer oaths to witnesses testifying in evidentiary hearings (these oaths to tell the truth can also be administered by the clerk to the board). Also, the chair rules on requests that the board issue subpoenas to compel testimony or the production of evidence.

In addition, the chair serves as the presiding officer at meetings. The chair is generally responsible for opening meetings and hearings, explaining the rules of participation to attendees, admonishing witnesses at evidentiary hearings to stick to the presentation of legally relevant evidence, and reminding board members to focus deliberations on relevant standards for decision. Chapter 4, on conducting evidentiary hearings, discusses these duties in more detail.

---

18. G.S. 160A-388(f) & (g).

# Chapter 3
# **Prior to the Evidentiary Hearing**

In advance of the evidentiary hearing the board and staff must follow certain steps and address specific issues. Proper notice of the public meeting and the evidentiary hearing must be provided. The preliminary record—including application, staff analysis, and other documents—must be compiled, distributed, and reviewed. Board members must consider any potential partiality, such as bias or conflicts of interest. Also, board members must be wary of communicating about the case outside of the hearing.

## Open Meetings and Public Records

To start, it is necessary to give an overview of the open meetings and public records requirements, as a board making a quasi-judicial decision is a public body subject to them.[1]

A public meeting occurs anytime a majority of the board gathers, in person or electronically, to conduct public business. So, whenever a board is holding an evidentiary hearing, deliberating and voting on a decision, or otherwise acting as a board, it must do so in open session open to the public. The board or the board's staff must create and retain full and accurate minutes of any public meeting. Social occasions where a majority of the board will be present are not public meetings, but the board must not discuss cases or otherwise conduct public business at such events.

The local government must provide notice of public meetings, and the schedule for regular meetings must be filed with the city or county clerk and posted to the website. Separate notice requirements apply to special

---

1. The statutory requirements for public meetings are outlined in G.S. Chapter 143, Article 33C, and the statutory requirements for public records are outlined at G.S. Chapter 132. For more details on these topics, see Frayda S. Bluestein & David M. Lawrence, Opening Meetings and Local Governments in North Carolina: Some Questions and Answers (8th ed. 2017) & David Lawrence, Public Records Law for North Carolina Local Governments (2009).

meetings, emergency meetings, and recessed meetings. Quasi-judicial evidentiary hearings require additional notice (discussed below).

A board making a quasi-judicial decision must deliberate and decide in open session. A public board may go into closed session only in limited circumstances, such as to protect attorney–client privilege or to discuss economic development incentives. It is rare for such a circumstance to apply to a board making a quasi-judicial decision; a board may go into closed session for the narrow purpose of obtaining legal advice from the board's attorney concerning statutory authority and legal requirements. Before a board goes into closed session it must specify the purpose and adopt a motion to go into closed session while in open session. The minutes of the closed session must provide a general account of the meeting. The closed session must be limited to privileged legal consultation; board deliberations and decision-making must be in open session.

A public record is any record made or received in the transaction of public business. Public records are subject to disclosure upon proper request unless an exception applies. An item can be a public record regardless of its format (electronic or hard copy) or location. An email concerning a quasi-judicial case, for example, is a public record regardless of whether it is on a government email account or a personal email account. The following are public records that would be subject to disclosure: emails about a quasi-judicial decision sent to a board member; a text message from a board member to a staff person about an upcoming case, application materials, and notes from a meeting between the applicant and staff; and any written correspondence among board members regarding the board's business.

## Application and Timing

The local government should have application forms to facilitate requests for the various quasi-judicial decisions. Application forms should set forth the ordinance standards and solicit the information needed to make a decision. Through the application and related documents, the applicant should

- provide evidence and argument to support the applicant's case,
- properly allege standing,
- provide evidence or certification supporting the authenticity of any documentary evidence, including photographs and documents.

Once an individual has properly filed a request for a quasi-judicial decision, the board should hear the case within a reasonable time (the ordinance may specify a time frame). Once a complete application is filed properly, staff is obligated to put the request on the agenda for the board; staff cannot make decisions on legal questions, such as standing.[2]

A board may establish reasonable standards for the timing of submission of materials so that there is sufficient time for review by staff and the board in advance of the hearing. Once the hearing is scheduled, a party may request that it be delayed. The board may allow such delay but is not obligated to do so. If additional or amended materials are provided, the board may choose to delay the hearing to a subsequent meeting.

A local government may charge a reasonable application fee to offset the costs of hearing notices, application review, and related costs. A sample application form is presented in Appendix A.

## Notice

In addition to the general notice requirements required for public meetings, quasi-judicial evidentiary hearings have specific requirements for mailed notice and posted notice.[3] Notice of the hearing must be mailed at least ten days prior to but not more than twenty-five days prior to the hearing. The rules for counting days state that the day of publication is not counted in computing these times, but the day of the hearing is included. Notice is mailed to the following:

- the applicant,
- the owner of the subject property (if different from the applicant),
- the owners of land abutting the subject parcel,
- any other individuals entitled to notice under the ordinance.

The local government also must prominently post a sign on the subject property or adjacent right-of-way to notify passersby of the upcoming hearing. The sign must be posted during the window of time for mailed notice—at least ten days but not more than twenty-five days prior to the hearing.

---

2. Morningstar Marinas/Eaton Ferry, LLC v. Warren Cty., 368 N.C. 360, 360, 777 S.E.2d 733, 734 (2015).

3. G.S. 160A-388(a2).

These notice requirements are the minimum required by state law, and many local governments adopt additional notice requirements. Some local ordinances require mailed notice for any property within a certain distance of the subject property (100 feet, for example) and not merely for abutting parcels. There is no state requirement for newspaper published notice, but some local ordinances call for published notice. The local government must adhere to any locally adopted notice requirements in addition to the basic requirements of state law.

Although not explicitly required by state law, the notice should include basic information about the case, including the name of the applicant, address of the property, nature of the application, time and place of the hearing, and contact information for local government staff. Most neighbors and interested citizens are unfamiliar with quasi-judicial procedures. The local government website and/or written materials can provide some guidance for participating in a quasi-judicial hearing. Mailed notice can include a basic statement about the type of hearing and how neighbors can participate, such as the following.

> This type of decision requires a quasi-judicial hearing. The applicant must show that the project meets certain standards, including [list the applicable standards]. The board must base its decision on factual testimony, not general public opinion. To learn more about how you can participate in the hearing, please [see website or contact planning office].

A sample hearing notice letter is presented as Appendix B.

## Preliminary Record

Some elements of the record are compiled in advance of the evidentiary hearing. The applicant should provide an application and supporting documentation to thoroughly explain the request and to support the applicant's case. Staff analysis of the application materials and applicable standards also provides critical information for evaluating the request.

This preliminary record—application, applicant's supporting documentation, any staff analysis and related materials—should be prepared and distributed to the board and the parties a reasonable time in advance of the hearing so that those individuals have an opportunity to review. The preliminary record may be available electronically or in hard copy at the local government. For appeals of staff decisions, state law requires the staff person to compile the record and provide it to the board and appealing party (discussed in detail in Chapter 9).

Board members should review the application materials and staff analysis. A board member should not have a fixed opinion (that would be impermissible bias) but should be familiar with the specific request, the standards that apply, and the supporting evidence provided. Application materials and written staff analysis do not raise the underlying concerns of ex parte communication because they are available to all parties and may be challenged and rebutted at the hearing. As discussed below, any further discussions (beyond the written materials) may raise concerns of ex parte communication.

In some communities, staff creates a draft finding of fact and decision document in advance of the hearing. The draft, then, can be revised to reflect the evidence presented at the hearing, the deliberation of the board, and the final decision. This approach is discussed more in Chapter 5.

## Site Visits

Site visits can be extremely helpful for some cases. Special use permits, for example, often require that the project be "in harmony with the area." Board members need to be familiar with the area in order to determine what would be in harmony with it. While site visits may be prudent or even necessary, board members should adhere to some limits in order to ensure their safety and protect rights of the parties and others.

**Numbers matter.** A majority of the board being present at one time constitutes a public meeting that must be open to the public and for which public notice must be given. In order to avoid the process of conducting a formal public meeting, some boards avoid having a majority make a site visit at one time.

**Respect private property.** When board members can observe the character of an area from public streets and sidewalks, they will not need to go onto private property. Sometimes, however, it is necessary to go onto private property in order to observe the possible impacts of a proposed development. The impact on neighbors, for example, may not be evident from the public right-of-way, especially in the case of large tracts. In those circumstances when board members may need to visit the property, it is prudent for staff to coordinate the visit with the property owner in advance.

**Keep personal safety in mind.** Board members should make site visits during the day and should not wander on to private property without permission. Board members may visit in pairs (unless that constitutes a majority of the board).

**Avoid ex parte communication.** Site visits raise the risk of ex parte communication. For example, the owner may want to explain the proposal, or a neighbor may want to complain about the project. Board members should avoid such conversations and disclose any conversations that do occur. A possible response script is included in the section titled "Communications," below.

**Disclose site visit and any important observations.** During a site visit, a board member takes in evidence that may inform her or his decision. At the hearing, the board member should disclose that she or he made a site visit. If the board member made observations that might sway her or his decision on the issue, those also should be noted. There is no need for either detailed notes or a lengthy statement; a brief statement of observations is sufficient.

## Subpoenas

The chair of the board of adjustment is empowered to subpoena witnesses and compel the production of evidence, if necessary, though this power is rarely used.[4] A person with standing (a party) may make a written request for the issuance of a subpoena explaining why it is necessary. The chair issues requested subpoenas determined to be "relevant, reasonable in nature and scope, and not oppressive." The chair also rules on any motions to quash or modify a subpoena. A party may appeal the chair's decision on a subpoena to the full board of adjustment. If a person fails to comply with a subpoena, the board or the party seeking the subpoena may apply to the superior court for an order compelling compliance.

While the statute expressly addresses boards of adjustment, other boards likely have the same subpoena power when acting as quasi-judicial decision-makers. A sample subpoena is presented in Appendix C.

---

4. G.S. 160A-388(g).

## Impartiality

All parties in a quasi-judicial hearing have the constitutional right to be adjudged by an impartial decision-maker.[5] Thus, a board member who is biased or has a conflict of interest must not participate. Bias in a quasi-judicial matter is when a board member has "a fixed opinion prior to hearing the matter that is not susceptible to change"; a board member has a conflict of interest if he or she has "a close familial, business, or other associational relationship with an affected person, or a financial interest in the outcome of the matter."[6] Undisclosed ex parte communications (discussed below) also are impermissible violations of due process.

A board member who is concerned about his or her own impartiality or the impartiality of another board member is advised to consult with the local government attorney so that the issue can be addressed in advance of the hearing. As discussed in Chapter 4, the issue of impartiality may be raised during the hearing by a party or a board member. If a dispute arises as to whether or not a member should be recused, the remainder of the board votes to determine if that member is recused.

In addition to the constitutional and statutory standards for impartiality in quasi-judicial cases, the governing board is subject to a locally adopted code of ethics.[7] Appointed boards, such as the planning board or board of adjustment, may also be subject to a local code of ethics.

## Communications

Ex parte communication occurs when a board member communicates about the case outside of the evidentiary hearing. Examples of ex parte communication include a board member meeting with a developer; a board member taking a call from a neighbor; and an email conversation among board members in which they deliberate the merits of an upcoming application. A board member getting a briefing on the case with staff in advance of the evidentiary hearing also would amount to ex parte communication. Undisclosed ex parte communications are impermissible violations of the parties' constitutional due process rights.

---

5. G.S. 160A-388(e)(2); Cty. of Lancaster, S.C., v. Mecklenburg County, N.C., 334 N.C. 496, 434 S.E.2d 604 (1993).

6. G.S. 160A-388(e)(2).

7. G.S. 153A-53 & G.S. 160A-86.

Ex parte communications raise concern for multiple reasons. The first is fairness. If a board member hears information from one party or potential witness, the other party is not there to challenge the information and provide rebuttal. Second is quality decision-making. When a board makes a decision, all board members should have the same information upon which to base their decision. Third is potential bias. Undisclosed communications may indicate impermissible bias.

Board members must take steps to avoid communications with parties, witnesses, or the general public about the request under consideration. Emails from the neighbor should be forwarded for city staff to address. Conversations with interested community members (at the grocery store, for example) should be ended politely but directly with an invitation for that interested individual to address the entire board at the evidentiary hearing. Board members should avoid communications with each other about a particular case. Those communications should be reserved for deliberation during and at the conclusion of the evidentiary hearing.

Any ex parte communications that occur must be disclosed in the evidentiary hearing. And as discussed above, any record made or received in the transaction of public business is a public record and subject to disclosure, unless an exception applies. Any email, text message, letter, or other document sent to or from a board member and concerning a quasi-judicial case is a public record. It must be archived under records retention laws and is subject to disclosure, unless an exception applies.

Notably, the concern of ex parte communications is a concern about communications with the decision-maker—the board—and not about communications with staff. The applicant, other parties, and interested citizens can and should contact local government staff to access the materials, ask questions, and better understand the process.

---

### A POSSIBLE RESPONSE TO THE INTERESTED NEIGHBOR

"Thank you very much for your interest in this matter. It sounds like you have good information to share, and I want to be sure that the full board can hear from you. Please come to the hearing on [date and time] at [location]. There are strict procedures for this type of hearing, so you should check with the planning staff to learn more about the case and the procedures."

If the neighbor tries to continue the conversation, a possible response could be: "State law limits my conversations outside of the hearing, but I do hope you will attend the hearing."

# Chapter 4
# **Conducting the Evidentiary Hearing**

A board holds an evidentiary hearing in order to build and evaluate the record upon which it will make its decision. Throughout the process the board must respect the due process rights of the parties and adhere to specific procedural requirements.

## **Essential Elements of a Fair Trial**

When making a quasi-judicial decision the board must adhere to basic standards of a fair trial.[1] State law demands that the board must

- follow applicable procedures and conduct hearings in accordance with fair-trial standards;
- be an impartial decision-maker;
- allow parties with standing an opportunity to
  - present evidence,
  - cross-examine adverse witnesses,
  - inspect documents,
  - offer explanation and rebuttal;
- ensure that witnesses are sworn and that any opinion testimony is from qualified experts;
- base its decision on competent, material, and substantial evidence in the record;
- provide a written decision resolving any disputed material facts and stating the basic facts on which it relied.

Additional procedures and limits may be placed on the board by its rules of procedure. Boards holding quasi-judicial evidentiary hearings must adhere to any state requirements as well as any local rules.

---

1. Humble Oil & Ref. Co. v. Bd. of Alderman, 284 N.C. 458, 202 S.E.2d 129 (1974); G.S. 160A-388.

## Building the Record

State law demands that every quasi-judicial decision be based on "competent, material, and substantial evidence *in the record.*[2]" Without such evidence, the decision is arbitrary and an abuse of the discretion vested in the board.[3]

The record includes all documents, exhibits, and testimony submitted to the board. So the record includes the application; staff report; photographs, plans, and diagrams; studies and reports prepared by the applicant; exhibits presented by opposing parties; and the minutes of the evidentiary hearing. The evidentiary hearing may be taped (audio and/or video). There is no state requirement for taping, but many local governments do record evidentiary hearings as a matter of practice or as required by local ordinance or rule. On appeal to superior court the record may include a transcript of the hearing (prepared and paid for by the requesting party). If it is anticipated that a case may be appealed to court, the parties will sometimes arrange for a court reporter to record the hearing and prepare a verbatim transcript.

Given the nature of quasi-judicial proceedings, some material presented may be incompetent or immaterial. Examples would include general opposition emails from the neighbors, unqualified opinion, or irrelevant facts. This material may remain in the record but may not be the basis of the quasi-judicial decision. As long as the record includes competent, material, and substantial evidence to support the board's decision, the admission of other arguably incompetent or irrelevant material does not infringe upon the parties' due process rights.[4] As discussed in greater detail below, however, it is prudent for the board chair to limit the introduction of irrelevant and incompetent testimony and evidence.

---

2. G.S. 160A-388(e2)(1) (emphasis added).

3. Godfrey v. Zoning Bd. of Adjustment, 317 N.C. 51, 60, 344 S.E.2d 272, 278 (1986) (quoting Coastal Ready-Mix Concrete Co., Inc. v. Bd. of Comm'rs of the Town of Nags Head, 299 N.C. 620, 265 S.E. 2d 379 (1980)) (emphasis added). *See also* G.S. 160A-393.

4. Dobo v. Zoning Bd. of Adjustment of City of Wilmington, 149 N.C. App. 701, 709–10, 562 S.E.2d 108, 114 (2002), *rev'd on other ground*, 356 N.C. 656, 576 S.E.2d 324 (2003).

## Roles and Responsibilities
### Chair

The chair of the board serves as the judge presiding over the evidentiary hearing. The chair opens the hearing, proceeds through the agenda, and maintains decorum. The chair acts to keep discussion and deliberation focused on the applicable standards and the relevant evidence. Depending on the local rules of procedure, the chair may have a variety of other roles. The chair may administer the oath for witnesses, or that may be handled by an authorized staff person. The chair may rule on legal objections made by the parties, though those decisions also may be made by the full board. Typically, the chair is a voting member of the board.

### Board Members

Each board member carries the heavy burden of being a decision-maker. Board members should therefore prepare for the hearing by reviewing case materials provided by staff as well as the ordinance and the standards to be applied to the case and, when appropriate, make site visits. Board members can also seek out applicable procedural guidance, such as the board's rules of procedure and the contents of this book. Board members should not conduct independent factual research or an investigation (for example, board members should not independently investigate a case by searching the Internet).

Board members must conduct themselves fairly and with impartiality. During the hearing, board members listen attentively and ask questions for clarification. They assess the credibility and reliability of each witness. They respectfully test the evidence for relevance, competence, and substance. As a practical matter, most of the actual cross-examination at an evidentiary hearing comes in the form of questions from members of the board.

### Staff

From the start staff serves as primary contact for the applicant, the coordinator for procedural requirements, and the record-keeper. This includes processing the application and materials, compiling and labeling materials for the record, analyzing the application and drafting documents, and providing and certifying notice, among other things.

During the evidentiary hearing a local government staff member typically serves as clerk to the board. These duties potentially include swearing in witnesses; collecting, cataloging, and maintaining all documentary evidence; compiling the minutes; and providing other administrative support for the board.

It is common for a staff member to be the initial witness at an evidentiary hearing. The staff member testifies as to what the ordinance requires, summarizes the application received, and recounts any staff analysis or review of the application. Like any other witness, the staff member is to be sworn in and is subject to cross-examination by the applicant, any other party, and by board members who may have questions. In some communities the staff member also makes a recommendation on the decision or suggests conditions to be imposed, whereas in others he or she only presents factual information. Either approach is legally acceptable.

In appeals of staff decisions, the staff person acts more as a party to the case rather than as a clerk serving the board. This role is discussed more in Chapter 9.

In addition to planning staff, a local government attorney often is present to advise and assist the board with legal questions that arise in the course of the hearing. In cases of appeals to the board of adjustment (from decisions by staff or the preservation commission) multiple local government attorneys may be needed to represent the differing interests.

## Parties

Parties with standing have rights that must be respected through the evidentiary hearings. As discussed more below, these rights include an opportunity to present evidence, to cross-examine adverse witnesses, to inspect documents, to make motions and object to testimony and evidence, and to offer explanation and rebuttal.

An attorney may represent a party and act on the party's behalf during the hearing. A party, or the party's attorney, may call witnesses to provide testimony before the board. If an attorney testifies about the facts of the case, those facts are treated the same as those provided by any other witness, and the attorney should be placed under oath and be subject to cross-examination.

Based on an ethics opinion from the North Carolina State Bar, non-lawyers may not provide legal advocacy on behalf of a party.[5] Architects,

---

5. N.C. STATE BAR, *Quasi-Judicial Hearings on Zoning and Land Use*, Authorized Practice Advisory Opinion 2006-1 (Oct. 20, 2006).

engineers, surveyors, and other land use professionals certainly can participate as witnesses in a quasi-judicial hearing and provide critical evidence in support of their clients. Such actions as examining evidence, cross-examining witnesses, and making legal arguments come under the purview of the practice of law and must be performed by the party or the party's licensed attorney.

### Non-Party Witnesses

Boards commonly allow other individuals to participate as witnesses in evidentiary hearings. As discussed below, the board is not required to allow non-parties to offer relevant testimony, but the board may allow such participation. Like any other witness, the non-party individual must be sworn in and is subject to cross-examination by the applicant, any other party, and by board members who may have questions. An individual without standing does not have rights of a party, such as objecting to evidence or cross-examining others.

## Distinguishing Witnesses and Parties with Standing

The ability of an individual to participate in a quasi-judicial hearing as a witness is a related but separate issue from the rights of an individual to act as a party with legal standing.

### Acting as a Witness

Many different individuals serve as witnesses in an evidentiary hearing. Consider an evidentiary hearing for a conditional use permit. A member of the planning staff introduces the application and provides staff analysis of the project. The staff person does not have legal standing but nonetheless provides important evidence and analysis for the board. The applicant may call a variety of witnesses or experts to testify on his or her behalf. These individuals do not have individual standing, but they provide testimony and argument on behalf of the applicant, who clearly does have standing.

Many boards call other interested individuals as witnesses to provide sworn testimony even though they lack legal standing. The board is *not required* to allow those individuals without standing to participate, but the board *may allow* such individuals to serve as witnesses—to provide competent, relevant, and substantial evidence on the matter. Indeed, a board seeking to make the most informed decision may welcome additional competent, relevant, and substantial testimony.

## Acting as a Party with Standing

A party with standing is an aggrieved party who would suffer special damages from the outcome of the matter. Relatively few individuals have legal standing in the quasi-judicial decision, but those who do are distinct from the general public and enjoy certain due process rights that must be protected.

An individual must have standing to act as a party in appealing a staff decision (or preservation decision) to the board of adjustment, cross-examining witnesses, making motions or objections, challenging the impartiality of a decision-maker, and appealing a decision to superior court. Otherwise the proceedings could infringe on the constitutional due process rights of the individuals who do have standing in the matter.

State law outlines who has standing to appeal a quasi-judicial decision, and this guidance is instructive for determining standing in the initial quasi-judicial hearing.[6] The following having standing as a party:

- a person with a legal interest in the subject property (this includes ownership; lease interest; an option or contract to purchase the property; or an interest created by an easement, restriction, or covenant),
- the applicant before the decision-making board,
- the city or county when the governing board believes the decision was made in error,
- a person who will suffer special damages as a result of the decision (discussed more below),
- an association organized to promote the interests of a particular area (such as a homeowners association or community association) so long as at least one member would have standing as an individual and the association was not created in response to the development at issue.

---

6. G.S. 160A-393.

## TIMES TO CONSIDER STANDING

### On the Application

In order for an individual to bring a case before a quasi-judicial board, that individual must have standing as a party. The application form can and should ask the applicant to support his or her claim of standing. For a property owner seeking a variance it's easy: he or she owns the subject property. But for appeals by a neighbor of the subject property, the appealing neighbor should properly allege standing in order to be heard. The board can rule on the standing question at the start of the hearing.

### At the Start of the Hearing

For any quasi-judicial hearing a neighbor or other interested individual may wish to act as a party in opposition to the request. If the individual is identified in advance (from communications with staff or on a sign-up sheet at the hearing), the board may make a standing determination early in the hearing. The individual can be called to make a proper allegation of standing, and then the board can make a determination about the individual's legal standing.

### In the Middle of a Hearing

Occasionally an individual will want to start acting as a party in the middle of a hearing—challenging the board's impartiality, objecting to evidence, or cross-examining witnesses. Before the individual is allowed to take such actions, she or he needs to establish standing as a party. The board can rule on that individual's standing and then proceed with the hearing.

   If the board fails to make a formal ruling on standing but allows the party to act as a party, the board has ruled implicitly that the party has standing.

## Evidence of Special Damages

There is no simple test for standing. Rather, each case is a fact-specific inquiry based on a set of factors that includes proximity, property value, and other adverse impacts. The central question is this: Has the individual who alleges standing shown that his or her damages are distinct from those damages to the public at large? Following are some critical factors to consider:

   **Proximity.** While proximity "in and of itself, is insufficient to grant standing, it does bear some weight on the issue of whether the complaining party has suffered or will suffer special damages distinct from those damages to the public at large."[7]

**Property value.** "Usually, special damages include economic damages such as a decrease in property value and other direct adverse effects on the property. . . . "[8] Vague, general allegations of decreased property value are insufficient.[9]

**Secondary impacts.** The individual alleging standing must show secondary adverse impacts particular to his or her property. For example, impacts related by traffic, parking, security, stormwater runoff, littering, and noise may be key factors in depreciating property values. The essential element is a credible allegation of harm to the use and enjoyment of a particular property.

The individual claiming standing must make a credible allegation of special damages. The board must make a finding as to whether or not the individual will suffer special damages. If a board does not rule formally on the question of standing but allows an individual to proceed as a party, it has implicitly ruled that the party has standing.

---

7. Mangum v. Raleigh Bd. of Adjustment, 362 N.C. 640, 644, 669 S.E.2d 279, 283 (2008).

8. Cherry v. Wiesner, 781 S.E.2d 871, 874 (N.C. Ct. App. 2016), *review denied,* No. 103P16, 2016 WL 4468152 (N.C. Aug. 18, 2016).

9. Lloyd v. Town of Chapel Hill, 127 N.C. App. 347, 351, 489 S.E.2d 898, 900 (1997).

## SAMPLE SEQUENCE OF AN EVIDENTIARY HEARING

*Note: A sample Chair's script for leading an evidentiary hearing is provided at Appendix E.*

- Announce the case and open the evidentiary hearing.
- Explain the quasi-judicial nature of the case, the standards that apply, and the appropriate ways of participating.
- Swear all witnesses regarding the case.
- Call for disclosure by board members of any ex parte communication, bias, and conflicts of interest.
- Consider questions of standing (if contested).
- Chairperson or designee (staff) presents an overview of the case and formally enters preliminary materials into the record.
- Applicant/appealing party presents his or her case.
  - Witnesses may be called for testimony.
  - Additional documents may be entered into the record.
  - Board members may ask questions.
  - Other parties with standing may cross-examine.
- Other parties with standing present their case.
  - Witnesses may be called for testimony.
  - Additional documents may be provided and entered into the record.
  - Board members may ask questions.
  - Applicant/appealing party may cross-examine.
- Board calls other witnesses (if permitted by the board).
  - Witnesses are called for testimony.
  - Additional documents may be provided and entered into the record.
  - Board members may ask questions.
  - Applicant/appealing party may cross-examine.
- Applicant/appealing party makes his or her rebuttal argument.
- Other parties make their rebuttal arguments.
- Board deliberates the case (evidentiary hearing may be closed or may be left open for clarifying questions).
- Board makes a decision on the case.
  - Vote on findings and decision may be separate or combined.
  - Motion is made and seconded to grant, grant with conditions, or deny (Board may have draft motions from staff).
  - Vote is taken and recorded.

*(continued)*

---

**SAMPLE SEQUENCE OF AN EVIDENTIARY HEARING** *(continued)*

- Decision document is drafted and signed by the Chair (typically at a later date).
- Decision is delivered to the parties.
- Minutes of the meeting are approved at a future board meeting.

For large and complex cases, it may be useful to establish reasonable ground rules in advance to protect the rights of the parties and to avoid an unnecessarily prolonged hearing. Such rules may include stipulating agreeable facts, establishing reasonable order and time guidelines, identifying the exhibit list and witness list in advance, and encouraging parties with similar interests to coordinate their evidence and argument.

---

## Opening a Hearing

### Nature of the Decision

At the start of an evidentiary hearing it is useful for the chair to explain the nature of the decision—a quasi-judicial decision based on evidence in the record. It is important to distinguish this decision and process from the more familiar legislative zoning decisions where general public comment is encouraged and required. Clarifying the nature of the quasi-judicial hearing sets the stage for proper procedures: It reminds the board of the standards for the decision; it reminds the parties of their individual roles in the hearing; and for those individuals unfamiliar with quasi-judicial procedures, it provides a brief introduction.

---

**SAMPLE OPENING STATEMENT**

"This hearing is a quasi-judicial evidentiary hearing. That means it is like a court hearing. State law sets specific procedures and rules concerning how this board must make its decision. These rules are different from other types of land use decisions like rezoning cases.

"The board's discretion is limited. The board must base its decision upon competent, relevant, and substantial evidence in the record. A quasi-judicial decision is not a popularity contest. It is a decision constrained by the standards in the ordinance and based on the facts presented. If you will be speaking as a witness, please focus on the facts and standards, not personal preference or opinion.

"Participation is limited. This meeting is open to the public. Everyone is welcome to watch. Parties with standing have rights to participate fully. Parties may present evidence, call witnesses, and make legal arguments. Parties are limited to the applicant, the local government, and individuals who can show they will suffer special damages. Other individuals may serve as witnesses when called by the board. General witness testimony is limited to facts, not opinions. For certain topics, this board needs to hear opinion testimony from expert witnesses. These topics include projections about impacts on property values and projections about impacts of increased traffic. Individuals providing expert opinion must be qualified as experts and provide the factual evidence upon which they base their expert opinion.

"Witnesses must swear or affirm their testimony. At this time, we will administer the oath for all individuals who intend to provide witness testimony."

---

## Oath

Any person seeking to offer testimony in a quasi-judicial hearing must be sworn in.[10] This includes parties who will speak, local government staff who will present evidence, and other interested individuals who will speak. The chair of the board, any member acting as chair, or the clerk to the board may administer the oath. Anyone who willfully provides false testimony is guilty of a Class 1 misdemeanor. Oaths may be administered for all

---

10. G.S. 160A-388(f).

witnesses at the start of the hearing, or oaths may be administered individually for each witness. Either way, the practice should follow the local rules of procedure. Individuals who are unable or unwilling to swear may provide a solemn affirmation instead.

---

### OATH

A typical oath, based on the oath for witnesses in civil matters, is as follows:

Do you solemnly swear or affirm that the evidence you shall give to the board in this action shall be the truth, the whole truth, and nothing but the truth [so help you God]?

---

### Disclosures

A call for disclosures should be routine. The board should have a standard point on the agenda or procedure to call for board member disclosures of conflicts of interest, bias, and ex parte communication.

For conflicts of interest and bias, after a board member has identified the reason for partiality, that member should recuse herself or himself and step down from the dais. The issue of impartiality may also be raised by another board member or by a party. If there is a dispute as to whether or not a member should be recused, the remainder of the board votes to determine if the member is recused.

A recused board member should not participate in questioning, deliberation, or voting. At the very least the recused member should leave the area where the board is sitting and sit with the general public. Nonverbal communication can be powerful, though, so it may be appropriate for recused members to leave the room entirely for both the evidentiary hearing and decision.

In addition, it is inappropriate for a board member to participate in a hearing before the board on behalf of a client, friend, or family member. In very rare circumstances a board member may be a party and have due process rights to participate in the hearing.

Ex parte communication should be avoided. Board members should not confer with the parties or conduct independent factual research (aside from permissible site visits, when appropriate). In those circumstances when ex parte communication occurs, however, a board member should identify the communication, the basic information conveyed, and any specific information that may inform the board's decision. Site visits should be disclosed. Emails or other correspondence sent to board members should be referenced and included in the record.

Additional details of conflicts, bias, and ex parte communication are discussed in Chapter 3.

## Testimony
### Order of Presentation
The specific order for a quasi-judicial hearing will depend on the local rules of procedure and policies of the board. A common approach is as follows:

- staff presentation,
- applicant's testimony and argument,
- other parties' testimony and argument,
- other witness's testimony.

### Case Introduction
Typically staff will introduce the case, summarizing the request, stating the applicable standards, reciting notice provided, stating what materials were provided to the board in advance, and summarizing content of any staff analysis. This serves to formally introduce the application and staff analysis into the record.

## SAMPLE CALL FOR DISCLOSURES

"The parties to this case are entitled to an impartial board. A board member may not participate in this hearing if she or he has a fixed opinion about the matter, a financial interest in the outcome of the matter, or a close relationship with an affected person. Does any board member have any partiality to disclose and recusal to offer?"

*PAUSE*

*IF THERE IS A RECUSAL*

"It is the policy of this board that a recused member shall step down from the dais and _____ [insert "have a seat with the general public"; "be excused from the room"; or other policy]. The board member may return to the dais for the next matter."

*PROCEED TO EX PARTE COMMUNICATION*

"The parties to this case have rights for any ex parte communication to be disclosed. Ex parte communication is any communication about the case outside of the hearing. That may include site visits as well as conversations with parties, staff, or the general public. Does any board member have any site visits to disclose?"

*PAUSE*

"Does any board member have any conversations or other communications to disclose?"

*PAUSE*

"Based on the disclosures we've heard from the board concerning partiality and ex parte communications, does any member of the board or any party to this matter have an objection to a board member's participation in this hearing?"

*PAUSE*

*IF NOT, PROCEED WITH HEARING*

*IF A PARTY RAISES AN OBJECTION*

"_____ [insert party] has objected to _____'s [insert board member's name] participation in the hearing based on _____ [insert basis of objection]. When there is an objection to a board member participating in a quasi-judicial decision, the dispute is resolved by a majority vote of the remaining members of the board. I'll now ask the remaining members of the board for a motion as to _____'s [insert board member's name] participation in this hearing."

## Limits on Witnesses

Testimony from witnesses must be sworn, factual, and material. The chair should redirect or cut off testimony that is mere opinion, immaterial, or repetitive. While the board cannot set strict time limits on a party making his or her case, reasonable time guidance may be useful to help keep the parties and witnesses on task.

**Sworn.** Speakers offering testimony must be sworn in. As noted above, speakers may be sworn in as a group at the start of the hearing.

**Factual.** The whole point of the evidentiary hearing is to build and evaluate the record—to take in factual evidence on which to base a decision. Speakers should provide factual testimony, not personal opinion. There is limited allowance for expert opinions, as discussed below.

**Material.** The board must base its decision on the proposed development and the standards. Testimony must be focused on those material elements: the application and the standards. Other considerations—such as the character of the applicant, the politics for or against the proposal, and matters unrelated to the proposal—are beyond the board's authority.

**Non-repetitive.** In contrast to a public hearing (like for a rezoning), the board cannot set strict time limits on parties at a quasi-judicial evidentiary hearing. Board rules of procedure may set forth general time periods for testimony and cross-examination, but parties with standing have a right to be heard, so they must be given an opportunity to present evidence and argue their case. That right, though, is not a right to filibuster—they cannot hold the floor and prevent action.

## Personal Knowledge of Board Members

Board members may have personal knowledge or expertise relative to a pending case. They may have prior knowledge about conditions on the site or professional expertise about an issue under consideration. It is permissible for the board member to use this knowledge, but it is important that the member state that information for the record during the evidentiary hearing. This allows other board members to be aware of and consider that information as well as give the parties an opportunity to rebut or clarify that evidence.

---

**SAMPLE LIMIT ON WITNESS TESTIMONY**

"As a reminder, witnesses should provide factual testimony as to how this project does or does not meet the standards. The board must base its decision upon evidence in the record. Not personal preference or opinion.

"Please be aware that the applicant and any other parties have certain rights to object to your testimony and cross-examine you as a witness. The board, though, will determine what evidence to consider and how much weight to assign it."

*FOR OPINION TESTIMONY*

"As a reminder, your testimony must be focused on factual evidence concerning the applicable standards. This board must base its decision on factual evidence in the record, not personal opinions."

*FOR REPETITIVE TESTIMONY*

"The board appreciates your testimony. Other witnesses have already introduced this information into the record. Unless you have different evidence, we will have to move on to the next witness."

---

## Expert Opinion

A qualified expert is needed for technical matters concerning professional expertise. State law gives examples of what kinds of experts may be needed. These including the following:[11]

- A qualified appraiser to provide an expert opinion about whether and how a proposal will affect neighboring property values,
- A qualified transportation engineer to provide expert opinion about whether and how a proposal will increase traffic and pose a danger to public safety.

In order to provide expert opinion an individual must be established as an expert by his or her education, certification, and/or experience. Once an individual provides evidence to support his or her status as an expert, other parties have a right to cross-examine the individual and present opposing

---

11. G.S. 160A-393(k)(3).

evidence. A local government staff person also should be qualified as an expert when she or he provides professional opinion testimony.

A board or chair of the board (depending on the local rules of procedure) should make a ruling on whether an individual is qualified as an expert. A party may object to this ruling. Such an objection may trigger a vote by the full board (if the chair alone ruled before) or preserve the issue for appeal to superior court.

Even if an individual is qualified as an expert, he or she still must substantiate the expert opinion provided through sufficient data and reliable methods. For example, the traffic engineer needs to provide the traffic analysis performed, and the appraiser needs to show the analysis used to establish the expert opinion about impacts to property values.

The line between permissible non-expert testimony and impermissible non-expert opinion is not always clear. Non-expert witnesses may provide factual testimony relating to the non-technical standards. A neighbor, for example, may provide maps, photographs, and testimony to address the question of whether a development is in harmony with the area. Similarly, a neighbor may provide relevant sections of the local comprehensive plan to address the question of whether a development is consistent with it. A neighbor speaking as a witness may testify about traffic jams he or she has seen, but that neighbor cannot offer an opinion about the impacts of possible increases in traffic from the proposed development unless that neighbor is a qualified transportation engineer. These distinctions are explored further in the sidebar titled "Evidence Examples" in Chapter 5.

### Cross-Examination

Parties in a quasi-judicial hearing have due process rights to cross-examine witnesses and offer rebuttal testimony. But, because quasi-judicial hearings generally lack the formal structure of a courtroom, cross-examination can pose some practical difficulties. The chair of the board must carefully manage this process to protect rights while maintaining decorum. The board itself provides a level of cross-examination of witnesses through its questioning, but parties have an independent right to cross-examine the witnesses. In order to facilitate cross-examination, some communities have parties that are not represented by an attorney direct their cross-examination questions to the board chair. The chair, in turn, asks the questions of the appropriate witness.

In any event, if it appears there will be a substantial amount of cross-examination from multiple parties, the board can establish reasonable procedures to allow that questioning in a fair, efficient and non-repetitive fashion.

## Documentary Evidence

The record in a quasi-judicial case generally includes documentary evidence, such as maps, drawings, reports, or photographs. Staff should mark and catalog evidence for ease of reference. If a witness is testifying about a particular document or photograph, it is helpful if the record clearly reflects which document is involved (such as, "As shown on the map labeled Exhibit 3 . . . "). The record will be retained indefinitely, so if parties desire to introduce valuable documents (e.g., the 1930s family photo of the old house), they should provide a copy of the original.

As discussed below, there is some allowance for evidence in quasi-judicial hearings that does not meet the strict rules of evidence required in a courtroom. Even so, the board needs assurance that the evidence is sufficiently trustworthy to reasonably be relied upon. The board, for example, needs assurance of the authenticity of the documents. A document may be authenticated if it is

- certified as authentic by the custodian of the record,
- confirmed as authentic by sworn testimony of a witness who has first-hand knowledge.

A photo may be authenticated by sworn testimony as to the date, the place where the photograph was taken, and that the photograph fairly and accurately represents the subject depicted at the time the photograph was taken.

Documents or photographs may be preserved in the record, even if they are not properly authenticated.

Board rules commonly specify the number of copies of a document to be submitted.

## Continuation of Hearing

The board may continue the hearing to a later date. The need for continuation may arise in a few different circumstances. A party may be ill, a key witness may be unavailable, or an applicant may need additional time to prepare. For large and complex cases, the board may need multiple days to hear all of the testimony. Boards generally make an accommodation for good cause, but a board is not obligated to continue the hearing.

There is no need for additional notice for the continued hearing if, during the initial hearing, the board announces the time and place where it will occur.

## Closing the Evidentiary Hearing

After the parties and interested individuals have provided testimony, the board shifts to deliberation, consideration of conditions, and voting (discussed in greater detail in the next chapter). Some boards leave the evidentiary hearing open during deliberation and voting in case the members need to ask clarifying questions of the parties.

Once the hearing is closed the board may not take in new evidence. The board may deliberate but may not take in new facts regarding the standards. If the hearing is closed and the board wants to take in more evidence, the board must provide notice to the parties to re-open the evidentiary phase of the hearing. This is not a problem if it takes place at the same meeting and the parties are still present, but it may be an issue if the board deliberates at a later date.

# Chapter 5
# Making a Decision

When a board makes a quasi-judicial decision it must do two things.

First, the board must *determine the facts* of the case. That is, the board must review all of the evidence that has been submitted, resolve competing evidence, and then decide the facts to be applied. Determining the weight of competing evidence is one of the critical jobs in making a quasi-judicial decision.

Second, the board must *apply the relevant standards* to those facts. In other words, the board must decide whether there is sufficient evidence in the record to determine whether or not each of the applicable standards has been met.

## Deliberation

After gathering the relevant factual evidence, a board making a quasi-judicial decision moves to consider the facts and how to resolve the case. In North Carolina, the board must not only take evidence in public; it also must deliberate and decide the case in open session.[1] While the board does not accept comments from observers once it concludes the evidentiary hearing, the board's deliberations and decision-making must be done in full public view. The board may not retreat to the jury room or a conference room for deliberations.

The law does allow a few narrow exceptions to the open meetings requirement.[2] Most of the permissible purposes for a closed session deal with contract and personnel matters and are not relevant for quasi-judicial decisions. One that may occasionally arise is the need to secure privileged legal advice from the board's attorney in order to protect the attorney–

---

1. G.S. 143-318.10.
2. G.S. 143-318.11.

client privilege (on such substantive issues as the scope of the board's statutory authority and potential constitutional issues).[3]

---

**OPENING DELIBERATION**

"We will now begin deliberation of this request. As a reminder this board is tasked with deciding if, based on the evidence presented, this proposal meets the applicable standards. This decision cannot be based on the personal preference of board members. Rather it is based on standards and evidence.

"Board members are encouraged to reference the applicable standards and specific evidence in their deliberation.

"For this particular case, the board is asked to decide: Does the record include competent, relevant, and substantial evidence that [insert standards for the request]?"

---

In light of the limitations placed on board deliberations, the following are some dos and don'ts:

- Don't offer comments framed as personal opinions (e.g., that begin with "I like . . . ," "I don't like . . . ," or "I feel . . . .").
- Do frame comments and deliberations with applicable facts and standards ("Based on the testimony from Mrs. Smith . . . "; "Based on design guideline 7b . . . ").
- Avoid redesigning a project by committee.
- Do offer direct comments about how a project does or does not meet local land use standards ("With regard to harmony with the area . . . "; "As designed, this project is not congruous with the district because . . . ").

---

3. Carolina Holdings, Inc. v. Hous. Appeals Bd., 149 N.C. App. 579, 585–86, 561 S.E.2d 541, 545, *review denied*, 356 N.C. 298, 570 S.E.2d 499 (2002).

## Burdens of Evidence

Who must produce the evidence needed to show whether the applicable standards are or are not met?

State law requires the applicant to produce sufficient evidence to show that the standards required for approval will be met.[4] It is not the job of the staff or the board to produce this evidence. It is the burden of the person seeking approval to do so. If the applicant fails to produce sufficient evidence that the standards will be met, the permit must be denied.[5] The unique scenario of staff interpretations is discussed in Chapter 9.

If the applicant produces sufficient evidence that the standards have been met and no substantial evidence is presented to the contrary, the applicant is entitled to the approval being sought.[6] In this situation the board must approve the application.

Once the applicant meets the burden of producing evidence that the applicable standards have been met, the burden then shifts to any opponents to produce contrary evidence sufficient to show that the standards have not been met. If opponents present substantial evidence that the standards have not been met, the board must decide which of the conflicting evidence is correct and make findings of fact to resolve that question.[7]

The board makes its decisions about whether these burdens are met based on the evidence properly presented before the board. A party will sometimes realize at the hearing that sufficient evidence to meet this burden has not been presented and will then ask for a chance to do so at a later date. The board has the discretion of continuing an evidentiary hearing if it wishes to allow additional evidence to be submitted, but the board is not required to grant such a request.

4. Humble Oil and Refining Co. v. Chapel Hill, 284 N.C. 458, 468, 202 S.E.2d 129, 202 (1974). See Chapter 7 for additional specialized considerations regarding the burdens when a special use permit is being considered.

5. Signorelli v. Town of Highlands, 93 N.C. App. 704, 379 S.E.2d 55 (1989).

6. Howard v. City of Kinston, 148 N.C. App. 238, 246, 558 S.E.2d 221, 227 (2002).

7. AT&T Wireless PCS, Inc. v. Winston-Salem Zoning Bd. of Adjustment, 172 F.3d 307 (4th Cir. 1999).

## Evaluating the Evidence

How much evidence must be produced for either the applicant or the opponents to meet their burden?

Unlike in criminal cases, the board does not have to determine the facts beyond a reasonable doubt. Instead, the courts have said that, in quasi-judicial matters, the board's findings of fact must be supported by "competent, material, and substantial evidence."[8] As previously mentioned, a decision that is not supported by substantial evidence in the record is deemed arbitrary and will be invalidated if challenged in court.[9]

Evidence is "competent" if it is sufficiently trustworthy and reliable, that is, legally fit and acceptable for consideration by the board. Has the witness sworn to tell the truth? Does the witness have first-hand knowledge of the matter being adjudicated? The evidence may not be deemed competent also because the courts have said it may not legally be relied upon. For example, when a provision of an ordinance is being interpreted, the recollection of the board's staff or of an individual member of the governing board as to the provision's purpose or intended construction is not competent evidence.[10]

Evidence is "material" if it shows that one of the standards to be applied will or will not be met. If the standard at issue is the impact of a project on property values, facts that have no bearing on property value impacts are not material. For example, in a special use permit case where the board is considering the property value impacts of a proposed fast-food restaurant, evidence about the health impacts of its offerings is not material. Similarly, if the board is considering the potential property value impacts of a proposed day care center, testimony about the town's need for an additional day care center is not material.

Evidence is "substantial" if it is relevant and something a reasonable mind would regard as sufficient to support a specific conclusion.[11] In this context, the issue is whether the totality of the evidence received could reasonably support the conclusions reached by the board. The opposite of substantial evidence would be "mere speculation," "unsubstantiated fears," or "vague assertions." In some instances the evidence presented could also support different conclusions. In such a circumstance, the reviewing court

---

8. *Humble Oil*, 284 N.C. at 468, 202 S.E.2d at 202.

9. Godfrey v. Zoning Bd. of Adjustment, 317 N.C. 51, 60, 344 S.E.2d 272, 278 (1986).

10. Fort v. Cty. of Cumberland, 218 N.C. App. 401, 408, 721 S.E.2d 350, 355 (2012).

11. C G & T Corp. v. Bd. of Adjustment, 105 N.C. App. 32, 40, 411 S.E.2d 655, 660 (1992).

will not substitute its judgment as to which conclusion is "right." Rather, the court will ask whether there is enough evidence in the record to allow a reasonable person to come to the same conclusion reached by the board.

Chapter 4 offers additional discussion on the procedures for keeping witnesses focused on providing competent, relevant, and substantial evidence.

The board considers all of the evidence properly presented to it—the application and supporting materials, staff reports, and other documents in the hearing record; site visits; as well as the testimony of all of the witnesses at the hearing. The board must not consider any evidence or information that is not properly included in the hearing record or that is presented after the evidentiary hearing has been closed.

### (Quasi-) Rules of Evidence

Courts have strict rules of evidence. Quasi-judicial boards must follow those rules—sort of. North Carolina courts allow some degree of informality for these citizen boards. State law allows that evidence that would not be admissible under the strict rules of evidence may be admissible for a quasi-judicial evidentiary hearing if: "(i) the evidence was admitted without objection or (ii) the evidence appears to be sufficiently trustworthy and was admitted under such circumstances that it was reasonable for the decision-making board to rely upon it."[12]

Hearsay is a prime example of this principle. Generally, a person needs to be present at the evidentiary hearing in order to testify. This allows the board to ask questions and judge the credibility of the person testifying and the parties to cross-examine and rebut that information. However, North Carolina courts have allowed boards to admit and consider a special class of hearsay evidence without the author being present: technical reports from experts and analyses by government officials. Examples from North Carolina case law include a letter from a state agency official, a technical report from a civil engineer, and a written comment from a school superintendent concerning school capacity.[13] Such statements and reports should be included in the record, not merely referenced in testimony.

---

12. G.S. 160A-393(k)(3).

13. Whiteco Outdoor Adver. v. Johnston Cty. Bd. of Adjustment, 132 N.C. App. 465, 513 S.E.2d 70 (1999); Harding v. Bd. of Adjustment, 170 N.C. App. 392, 612 S.E.2d 431 (2005); Tate Terrace Realty Investors, Inc. v. Currituck Cty., 127 N.C. App. 212, 488 S.E.2d 845 (1997), *review denied*, 347 N.C. 409, 496 S.E.2d 394 (1997).

Other hearsay evidence, however, is less credible. General letters, emails, and reported statements from individuals who are not present are examples. Such hearsay evidence may be included in the record, but the board cannot make critical findings of fact based solely on hearsay evidence.

## Making Factual Findings

One of the critical roles of a board making a quasi-judicial decision is determining the facts of the case. Much like a jury in a civil or criminal case, the board hears the evidence and decides the facts.

This is relatively easy if the facts are uncontested. If the applicant, the staff, and other affected parties all agree on the facts, the board simply needs to assure that those facts are indeed properly in the hearing record and affirm that they concur with them as stated. The board will decide later if the facts are substantial enough to show that the standards have or have not been met.

If the facts are contested, the board weighs the competing evidence and decides which is true and correct. The board's findings of fact must be reduced to writing and conveyed to the parties in a decision document. It is appropriate for the board to consider the sufficiency and reliability of evidence offered and the credibility of witnesses.

The board can ask for or allow the affected parties to submit proposed findings of fact for board review, modification, and approval. If that is done, the board must assure that there is evidence in the record to support the findings that are approved. Perhaps more common, especially in less populous jurisdictions, these findings are prepared by the staff or board's attorney after the meeting and then approved by the chair or by the board at its next meeting. A sample order that includes findings of fact and a decision for a simple variance is set out on pages 62 and 63.

## EVIDENCE EXAMPLES

Contrast the examples below. To the left is material on which the board cannot base its decision. To the right is evidence on which the board may base its decision.

| Material Not to Consider | Evidence to Consider |
|---|---|
| *From the applicant*: "As you can see in the drawings, this project is beautiful. The design, the details. It's exquisite." (*irrelevant opinion testimony*) | *From the applicant*: "As shown in the project drawings, the project is designed with a scale and massing similar to other buildings in the area." (*statement relevant to the standard of being in harmony with the area*) |
| *From a neighbor*: "We've seen how bad that motel on the other side of town is. There's bad folks there." (*unsubstantiated fears*) | *From a neighbor*: "Based on these police department statistics, similar uses in town have a high incidence of police calls." (*evidence to support potential safety concerns*) |
| *From a non-appraiser applicant*: "This project will not lower neighboring property values." (*unqualified opinion*) | *From a qualified appraiser with factual basis*: "In my expert opinion, this project will lower neighboring property values." (*expert opinion*) |
| *From a neighbor*: "This new project is going to drastically increase traffic. It's going to be dangerous." (*unqualified opinion*) | *From a neighbor*: "We already have substantial traffic along that road. It's hard to turn left at that intersection. And just this morning I saw a wreck there." (*factual statement; first-hand account*) |
| *From a concerned citizen, to the audience*: "Please stand up if you are here to oppose the project." [all of audience stands] (*public opinion*) | *From a concerned citizen*: "The land use plan calls for low-density residential for this property, but the proposal is for a substantial commercial operation." (*testimony related to applicable standards*) |

## Applying the Relevant Standards

At the outset of deliberations on a quasi-judicial matter, it is a good idea for the presiding officer or staff to state the standards for the decision. This helps remind the board members just what they will need to conclude and will help focus the deliberation and decision on relevant evidence.

So what are the standards the board must apply? There are several sources for the standards. State law sets out the mandatory standards to be applied for some types of decisions. A good example is a zoning variance, where state law requires the applicant to show the unnecessary hardship that would result without a variance and that the spirit and intent of the ordinance would still be met if the variance is granted. With special and conditional use permits, the zoning ordinance itself must specify the standards to be applied. With appeals of staff interpretations of the ordinance, the courts have supplied rules of construction that boards should use. Chapters that follow go into greater detail on the standards for each of these types of quasi-judicial decisions.

It is critical that the decision-making body limit itself to application of the standards set by law. Public opinion is irrelevant for quasi-judicial decisions. The question is whether the evidence supports a conclusion that the standards in the ordinance are or are not met. It is sometimes difficult for a board to vote against the wishes of a large contingent of concerned citizens. But a quasi-judicial decision is not a popularity contest. The board must fairly apply the standards in the ordinance regardless of popular opinion.

## Conditions

In addition to voting "yes" or "no" to a request for approval, the decision-making board has the option of imposing conditions on any approval it makes. The statutes specifically authorize imposition of "reasonable and appropriate conditions and safeguards" on special use permits,[14] "appropriate conditions" on any variance,[15] and "reasonable conditions necessary to carry out the purposes" of the ordinance on certificates of appropriateness

---

14. G.S. 153A-340(c1); G.S. 160A-381(c), -388(c).
15. G.S. 160A-388(c), (d).

in a historic district.[16] Conditions may be proposed by the applicant, the staff, neighbors, or a board member, but the decision on whether to include them is made by the board.

It is very common for conditions to be imposed as part of quasi-judicial decisions—a UNC School of Government survey found that about 90 percent of the state's cities and counties reported imposing conditions at least occasionally and that well over half reported doing so frequently.[17]

Conditions are acceptable if they are reasonably related to the proposed use, do not conflict with the ordinance, and further a legitimate objective of the ordinance.[18] Conditions also may insist on adherence to other relevant regulations, such as requiring that all necessary permits be obtained prior to construction.[19] In most instances, the conditions imposed are ones the board deems necessary to bring the project into compliance with the applicable standards. But it is not necessary to establish that the standards would be violated if not for the conditions. A condition that is reasonably related to furthering the objectives of a standard for decision can be imposed even if the project could meet the standard without the condition.[20]

The authority to impose conditions is not unlimited, however.[21] A board member cannot add a condition on a whim or to satisfy a personal preference. Conditions need to be related to the standards for approval, and evidence in the record should show that relationship. For example, if traffic impact is a relevant consideration and there is evidence in the record that the project as designed would create traffic problems, reasonable conditions can be added to the approval to prevent or minimize those problems.

---

16. G.S. 160A-400.9(a).

17. David W. Owens, Special Use Permits in North Carolina Zoning 17 (School of Government Special Series No. 22, Apr. 2007).

18. Overton v. Camden Cty., 155 N.C. App. 100, 104, 574 S.E.2d 150, 153 (2002).

19. Mangum v. Raleigh Bd. of Adjustment, 196 N.C. App. 249, 257, 674 S.E.2d 742, 748–49 (2009).

20. Nw. Prop. Group, LLC v. Town of Carrboro, 201 N.C. App. 449, 461–64, 687 S.E.2d 1, 9–11 (2009).

21. Crist v. City of Jacksonville, 131 N.C. App. 404, 405, 507 S.E.2d 899, 900 (1998).

## Motions

After the board has discussed the facts and their application to the relevant standards, it is time to vote. One of the members needs to make a motion to approve, approve with conditions, or deny the application. Standard motions can be prepared in advance by staff for use by board members. Some boards ask staff to prepare draft motions to approve and motions to deny on each case so that a board member can easily propose either course of action.

Some boards make a motion at the outset of the discussion, and the proceeding deliberation is of that motion. Other boards have an open discussion and deliberation before a member makes a motion on how to decide the case. Either approach is legally acceptable.

In some situations it is advisable to have multiple motions on which to decide a case. This arises both when there are contested facts that need to be resolved and when multiple standards need to be met.

When confronted with the issue of contested facts, many boards address their factual findings with a separate motion. While not legally required, this can help focus the board's deliberations. It also is very helpful to the court should the case undergo judicial review. For example, a special use permit application might be challenged by neighbors contending that the proposed project would have a "substantial adverse impact" on the value of their property. In such a case the board must determine what, if any, adverse impact would result and then whether that impact would be substantial. The permit could be granted because the board does not accept the neighbors' factual allegations about the impact on property values. Or it could be granted because the board accepts those factual allegations but concludes that the impacts are not substantial enough to violate the ordinance standard. Having one motion about the factual finding and a second motion about application of the standards can help clarify the board's decisions.

When multiple standards must be met, it is important for the board to be clear about which standards are or are not met. Requiring a separate motion and vote on each standard can help provide needed clarity. Boards also are allowed to consolidate the two motions into a single motion. A board that follows this process must take particular care to provide clarity. For example, a motion could state that "standards 1 through 4 have been met" or that "standards 1 through 3 are met but standard 4 is not met." In the latter occurrence, even if the board is denying the approval based on failure to meet standard 4, the board should specify that board members concluded that standards 1 through 3 have been met.

While not required by law, it is a useful practice to phrase motions in the affirmative when the decision to be made involves a variance. Because a four-fifth's majority of the board is required to approve a variance,[22] the vote calculation is less complicated if the motion is to approve. For this reason, some boards, and some rules of procedure for boards, require a motion to approve when a variance is requested. This way, the variance is issued only if the motion gets approval of four-fifths (or 80%) of the members eligible to vote (see the next section for more on voting and Chapter 6 for more on calculating the vote in variance cases). Should no member of the board actually be in favor of granting the variance, a member can, in this instance, make a motion to approve but then vote against it. This practice avoids the confusion that can arise with, for example, a tie vote on a motion to deny a variance; in that situation, the motion is not adopted because it did not receive a majority vote in favor, but the variance is denied nonetheless because it did not get a four-fifths majority of the board voting to grant it. It is thus advisable to always vote on a motion to approve the variance and see whether the motion gets four-fifths approval.

The discussion of the motion should be sufficiently detailed to allow production of the required written decision document. The decision needs to include not only the ultimate outcome—approval or denial—but also the rationale for that decision. This is true whether the application is approved or denied. The board must clearly indicate why it concluded that the standards were or were not met. After all, a denial may be challenged by the applicant and an approval may be challenged by the opponents. In either case, the parties and a reviewing court need to understand why the board decided as it did. So some explanation of the decision is required.

For example, a member might make a motion to deny a special use permit because although the evidence shows that the application meets all other standards, it fails to meet the standard on not creating adverse traffic impacts because it has only a single entryway and that entrance is so close to an existing busy intersection that it cannot safely handle the anticipated traffic in and out of the project site. The board's action needs to clearly show whether a majority of the board agree with that assessment or not.

The motion made at the hearing is different from the decision document discussed in the next chapter. Making and acting on a motion is the way the board makes its decision. That decision must later be reduced to

---

22. G.S. 160A-388(e). See Chapter 6 for more on variances.

writing, filed, and distributed to the parties. That is done with the decision document discussed below.

---

**SAMPLE MOTIONS**

**Motion to Approve**

Based on the testimony and hearing record before us, I move to find the pending application by Ms. Mary P. Smith for a special use permit to construct a 12-unit apartment building at 751 Main St. meets the four standards for special use permits set forth in Section 12.5 of the Mayberry Zoning Ordinance, provided the following two conditions are met: (1) the proposed driveway on Main Street is relocated 15 feet westward to avoid traffic conflicts at the intersection of Main and Elm Streets and (2) a fence at least 10 feet high is erected around the proposed dumpster at the rear of the apartment building in order to screen it from view from neighboring properties.

**Motion to Deny**

Based on the testimony and hearing record before us, I move to find that while the pending application by Ms. Mary P. Smith for a special use permit to construct a 12-unit apartment building at 751 Main St. meets standards 1, 2, and 4 for special use permits as set forth in Section 12.5 of the Mayberry Zoning Ordinance, the proposal fails to meet standard 3 of that section. Based on the testimony from the two appraisers regarding the significant adverse impacts on neighboring property values, standard 3 is not met, and the application for the special use permit is therefore denied.

---

## Voting

For most actions, a simple majority of the board is required. This is the case for decisions on special and conditional use permits, on appeals of staff determinations, on certificates of appropriateness, and on any quasi-judicial site plan or subdivision reviews.

The exception to this rule is a decision on a variance. Since a variance authorizes a landowner to act contrary to the express requirements of the ordinance, state law has always required a supermajority to grant a variance. A variance requires approval of four-fifths of the members of the entire board. This is discussed in greater detail in Chapter 6.

A question sometimes arises as to how to compute the required majority. The General Statutes specify how this is done. If a seat is vacant, it is not considered in the computation. If a member is recused and there is no alternate available to take that seat, that seat also is not considered in the computation. However, if a member is simply absent, that seat is counted. The statutes require "a majority of the members" of the board—not just a majority of those present and voting—to decide any quasi-judicial matter other than a variance.[23] The reason for the absence does not matter. For example, the seat of a member with an "excused" absence due to illness is still counted in the computation. Only vacant seats and seats of those recused on impartiality grounds are not considered in the computation.

What if membership on the board changes between the hearing and the board's vote? Or suppose a member was absent for the hearing but is present when the board deliberates and decides the case? In North Carolina, state law allows a member who was not present for the full hearing to vote on the case, provided that member has full access to the minutes of the hearing and all the evidence that was presented.[24] However, some local charters and ordinances disqualify a member who was not present for the entire hearing from voting on a quasi-judicial matter.

---

**VOTING CALCULATION**

Consider these examples on computing the majority needed to approve a special use permit. With a five-member board, a simple majority of three affirmative votes is required if all members are present and voting.

Suppose two members have a conflict of interest, there are no alternates available to replace those members, and the board votes 2–1 to approve the permit. Is it approved? Yes. Because the two members with a conflict cannot vote, the decision is made by a majority of the three members eligible to vote, making a 2–1 vote sufficient.

What if two members are simply not present? Would a 2–1 vote still result in approval of the permit? No. In this instance a majority of the full board is needed. Since there are no vacancies and no one has been excused due to a conflict of interest, a majority of five, or three affirmative votes, is needed to issue the permit. So, even though the vote is 2–1 in favor, the permit is denied.

For this reason, some ordinances and rules of procedure require or allow delaying a decision on a quasi-judicial matter until a full complement of eligible members are present and voting.

---

23. G.S. 160A-388(e).
24. Brannock v. Zoning Bd. of Adjustment, 260 N.C. 426, 132 S.E.2d 758 (1963).

## Precedent

A question sometimes arises about the impact of prior decisions. If the board last year made a special use permit decision on a project similar to one now under consideration, must the outcome be the same as that prior decision? Did the prior decision set a binding precedent?

It did not. Each individual case must stand on its own merits. Subtle differences in facts can lead to different results in similar cases.

That said, however, similar facts should generally produce similar results, assuming the ordinance provisions are still the same. If the facts of two cases are very similar and the board reaches a different result, it would be prudent for the board to explain why that is so.[25]

## Deadline to Make a Decision

North Carolina law does not specify a mandatory deadline for making a decision on most quasi-judicial decisions. The one exception to this general rule is that decisions on certificates of appropriateness for work in a historic district or on a landmark structure must be made within 180 days.[26] Except for these certificates, the General Statutes simply state that a decision must be made within a reasonable time.[27]

So what is "reasonable"? Sufficient time must be allowed to schedule a meeting of the board that makes the decision and to provide notice of the hearing. It is common for boards making these decisions to meet monthly, so the hearing is usually held a month or so after a complete application is in hand and the hearing can be properly advertised. Then the complexity of the case determines how long the hearing must be in order to receive all of the evidence. Most evidentiary hearings are completed in an hour or two, but a complex case can require multiple hearings conducted over several meetings. The parties sometimes request continuation of hearings due to schedule conflicts or the need for additional time to compile needed evidence. Given these varying circumstances, a simple case may be resolved in sixty to ninety days, while a more complex proceeding can easily take twice as long. So what is "reasonable" depends on the circumstances. What would

---

25. Through the Looking Glass, Inc. v. Zoning Bd. of Adjustment, 136 N.C. App. 212, 523 S.E.2d 444 (1999).
26. G.S. 160A-400.9(e).
27. G.S. 160A-388(e2).

be inappropriate, however, would be for a board to table a matter indefinitely or to make no effort to conclude the matter with a final decision.

It is legally permissible for a local ordinance to include a self-imposed deadline for decisions. For example, while not often done, a zoning ordinance could provide that decisions on requests for variances must be made within ninety days of receipt of a completed application, unless a continuance is requested by the applicant. If that provision is included, the ordinance also needs to spell out the consequences of failing to meet the deadline, such as deeming the application approved if no decision is made within the allotted time frame.

Once a decision is made, it is not effective until a written decision document is prepared, approved, filed, and delivered to the parties. This is discussed below. The same considerations regarding timeliness apply to the decision document.

## Decision Document

Decisions on quasi-judicial cases must be reduced to writing. On this point the General Statutes are explicit: "Each quasi-judicial decision shall be reduced to writing and reflect the board's determination of contested facts and their application to the applicable standards. The written decision shall be signed by the chair or other duly authorized member of the board."[28]

Most boards approve an order for each case that serves as the required formal decision document. This allows the action taken at the meeting to be written down, edited, verified and signed by the chair, and distributed in a timely fashion. A sample order that includes findings of fact and a decision for a simple variance is set out on pages 62 and 63. This is the process envisioned, if not explicitly required, by the statutes.

If the minutes are used as the formal decision document, the effective date of the decision and the time period for judicial review do not begin to run until the minutes are approved, signed, filed, and distributed—typically a month or more after the decision has been made.

This decision document should be distinguished from the oral motion made at the meeting (discussed in the previous chapter). The motion at the hearing determines the result. Ideally the motion should include some

---

28. G.S. 160A-388(e2)(1).

information on why the decision was reached, but motions are often rather sparse and do not capture the reasoning behind the board's decision. The written decision document reduces the decision to writing, explains how the evidence in the record led to that result, and generally contains more detail than the motion itself.

It is important that the decision document clearly set forth all of the reasons for the board's decision. If a decision is appealed to court, the court will only consider the grounds set forth for the decision document.[29] The board or its attorney cannot add additional grounds for the decision after the fact on appeal.

Some boards ask the parties or the staff to prepare draft decisions prior to the hearing. These are sometimes referred to as "proposed findings of fact and conclusions of law." Staff preparing these documents should consult as needed with the local government's attorney and avoid stepping beyond the preparation of staff documents and into giving the board legal advice. These proposed decisions can then be discussed, amended, and adopted by the board in its deliberations after receipt of evidence at the hearing. Of course, the evidence presented at the hearing would have to support any findings of fact in the proposed document. Having such a draft decision is permissible, but it is not required.

Typically the staff or the board's attorney prepares a written decision after the meeting that accurately reflects the action taken by the board. A few local governments offer the prevailing party the opportunity to draft the decision document, as is often done in court proceedings. In some jurisdictions, the board chair drafts the document.

It is important to note that a checklist showing that the board agrees the relevant standards were met or a conclusory statement avowing that the standards were met are not sufficient.[30] The checklist may be a valuable guide to the applicant as to what evidence is needed and may help focus board discussion of the matter but will rarely suffice as a decision document. The decision itself must show what the board concluded to be the essential facts of the case, how any contested facts were resolved, and how those facts establish that the relevant standards were or were not met.

---

29. Godfrey v. Zoning Bd. of Adjustment, 317 N.C. 51, 64, 344 S.E.2d 272, 279–80 (1986).

30. Clark v. City of Asheboro, 136 N.C. App. 114, 123, 524 S.E.2d 46, 52 (1999); Shoney's of Enka, Inc. v. Bd. of Adjustment, 119 N.C. 420, 458 S.E.2d 510 (1995).

The written decision must be sufficiently detailed to let the parties and a reviewing court understand the basis of the decision.[31]

When the written decision document is complete, the chair of the board reviews it to assure that it accurately reflects the board's decision. The chair (or other duly authorized member of the board) then signs the document. Some boards circulate the final draft to the full board and have a vote on adopting it at a subsequent meeting, whereas others delegate that review to the board chair.

---

31. Humble Oil and Refining Co. v. Bd. of Aldermen of Chapel Hill, 284 N.C. 458, 471, 202 S.E.2d 129, 138 (1974).

## SAMPLE FINDINGS OF FACT, DECISION, AND ORDER
### Variance Petition No. 2017-1

**Findings of Fact**

1. Helen Crump is the owner of a parcel located at 575 E. Front St. in Mayberry, N.C. The lot has 150 feet frontage on E. Front St. and a depth of 250 feet, as is shown on Attachment 1, the applicant's site plan. The lot is currently vacant.

2. The lot is currently zoned R-1 with required side-yard setbacks of fifteen feet.

3. There are wetlands along the east and rear portions of the lot, extending some 60 feet from the east property line. The wetlands are accurately depicted on Attachment 1.

4. On June 1, 2016, Helen Crump applied for a certificate of zoning compliance and building permit for a single-family residence at 575 E. Front St.

5. On June 7, 2016, Howard Sprague, town zoning inspector, denied the permit application of Helen Crump on the basis that the proposed structure would violate the side-yard setbacks on the west side of the property.

6. On June 15, 2016, Helen Crump submitted a complete petition for a variance of five feet from the side-yard setback requirement in order to locate a residence as depicted in Attachment 2, Crump's petition for a variance. This petition was assigned Case Number 2017-1.

7. On July 16, 2016, the Mayberry Board of Adjustment conducted a duly advertised and noticed evidentiary hearing on the Crump variance petition.

8. State and federal permit requirements prevent location of any residential structure on or over the wetlands depicted in Attachment 1.

(continued)

**SAMPLE FINDINGS OF FACT, DECISION, AND ORDER** (*continued*)

9. There is insufficient space on the lot to construct a residence of the size required by restrictive covenants and in a manner compatible with the surrounding property while avoiding the wetland area and meeting the side-yard setback.

10. If no residence can be constructed on the lot, there is no other practical use of the lot that has reasonable value.

11. Construction of a residence ten feet from the west side property line will not have a negative impact on the adjoining property.

12. Construction of a residence ten feet from the west property line will not impair emergency vehicle access, create a fire hazard, or otherwise be contrary to public health and safety.

**Conclusion and Decision**

1. Based on the application, the evidence submitted, and the above findings of fact, the board of adjustment by unanimous vote of 5–0 on July 16, 2016, concludes that Helen Crump meets each of the four standards set forth for a variance in Section 10.4 of the Mayberry Zoning Ordinance.*

2. Helen Crump is hereby granted a variance to construct a residence to be located ten feet from the west property line of her lot at 575 E. Front St., Mayberry, N.C.

3. This variance is conditioned upon a requirement that the ten feet between the residence depicted on Attachment 2 and the west property line be maintained as an undisturbed vegetated buffer.

4. This decision is effective upon distribution to the parties and filing with the clerk to the Board.

_____

Bernard Fife
Board Chair

Date of signature by chair: _____.

*For contested cases, many boards take the step of separately listing each relevant standard and noting how the evidence shows that each standard is or is not met.

---

**SAMPLE DECISION COVER LETTER**

To Applicant, Property Owner, and other Parties:

At its meeting on July 16, 2017, after conducting a duly advertised evidentiary hearing and after considering the application materials, testimony, and evidence presented at the hearing or otherwise appearing in the record, and the criteria set forth in Section 10.4 of the Town of Mayberry Unified Development Ordinance, the Mayberry Board of Adjustment voted 5–0 to **APPROVE** Helen Crump's petition for a side-yard variance at 575 E. Front St., based on the attached Findings of Fact and Conclusion and subject to the conditions set forth in the attached Order on Variance Petition 2017-1.

I, _____, Clerk to the Mayberry Board of Adjustment, do hereby certify the attached to be a true copy of the Order approved at the meeting of the Board of Adjustment held on July 16, 2017.

Date Filed with Clerk to the Board: _____

Date Mailed to Parties: _____

IN WITNESS WHEREOF, I have hereunto set my hand and have caused the seal of the Town of Mayberry to be affixed this the _____ day of _____, 2017.

_____
Clara Edwards
Clerk to the Board of Adjustment
(SEAL)

---

## Effective Date and Notice of Decision

The decision is not effective until the signed copy is filed with the clerk to the board.[32] A city or county ordinance may specify that the filing be with some other official, such as the city clerk or zoning administrator. It is important that the official receiving the filed decision clearly stamp it

---

32. G.S. 160A-388(e2).

with the date received, as this is the official effective date of the decision from which the time for appeals is measured.

A copy of the decision must then be delivered to the parties. A sample cover letter for the decision document is provided on page 64. A copy of the decision must be provided to

1. the applicant,
2. the property owner if that person was not the applicant, and
3. any other person who has submitted a written request for a copy prior to the effective date of the decision.

The law allows for delivery of the decision by email, first-class mail, or personal delivery.[33] The person who handles delivery of the decision is required to certify for the record that it has been delivered. This usually is done by the clerk signing an affidavit to be included in the case file that the decision was delivered on a specified date, indicating to whom it went and how it was delivered.

---

**CERTIFICATION OF DELIVERY OF DECISION DOCUMENT**

I certify that the above decision was filed with the clerk to the board of adjustment on _____, 2017, and mailed to the petitioner and each person making a written request for a copy of the decision at the hearing. The mailed copies were deposited in the U.S. mail with first-class postage affixed, addressed to the attached list of recipients, on _____, 2017.

_____

Clara Edwards
Clerk to the Board of Adjustment

---

33. *Id.*

## WHAT IS THE EFFECTIVE DATE OF THE DECISION?

Suppose the board has its hearing on a special use permit application on a Monday evening. After receiving testimony at the evidentiary hearing, the board discusses the case and votes that evening to issue the permit with a number of conditions. On Tuesday the board's attorney drafts a letter setting out the board's findings on contested facts and the conditions to be imposed. On Wednesday morning the board chair comes by the town offices, reviews the draft, and makes a few edits. That afternoon she stops by and signs the final decision document on behalf of the board. On Thursday morning the signed decision letter is filed with the board's clerk. The next day, Friday, the clerk emails a copy to the applicant and to the neighbors who had signed up at the hearing to get a copy of the decision. The following Monday the clerk drops a paper copy of the decision in the mail to the applicant and the neighbors.

The decision is effective on

- a. Monday, when the board voted;
- b. Wednesday, when signed by the chair;
- c. Thursday, when filed with the clerk;
- d. Friday, when e-mailed to the applicant; or
- e. The following Monday, when delivered to the post office.

The correct answer is Thursday, the day it was filed with the clerk to the board. All of the steps listed are essential and necessary, but the legal effective date of the decision is when it is filed. However, note that the thirty-day period to file for judicial review is the later of the effective date or the date it is delivered, which in this example would be Friday. If the decision was sent only by regular mail, not also by email, the time for judicial review would not start to run until three days after the Monday mailing.

## Hearing Record

Once a decision is made, the clerk to the board making the decision is responsible for maintaining the official hearing record. The material to be included in the record is all of the evidence that was considered by the board. (See the discussion in Chapter 4.) If the decision undergoes judicial review, the local government must compile the hearing record and provide it to the court for review, since the court considers whether the evidence properly before the board at the time of decision was sufficient. The hearing record provided to the court must be bound and paginated.

It also is important to retain the hearing record for use in administration and enforcement of the relevant ordinance. Issues may arise in future years as to exactly what was approved, the terms and conditions of approval, or precisely what was denied and why. Thus, many local governments retain the full hearing record on file indefinitely, at least in digital format. At a minimum the files must be retained as required by the state Division of Archives and Records retention schedule.[34] The current municipal and county schedules require permanent retention of the minutes of the board making the decision and retention of the quasi-judicial case files for six years.

## Rehearings

Once a quasi-judicial decision becomes effective, the board has no legal authority or jurisdiction to hear the same matter a second time.[35]

This rule is different from the question of rehearing a legislative matter. A city or county can take up the same legislative matter—a proposed rezoning or a text amendment—as often as it wishes. Many ordinances have self-imposed limitations on addressing the same legislative matter repetitively, such as the common requirement for a waiting period between rezoning petitions for the same parcel of land.

But the law is different for quasi-judicial matters because of the principle of res judicata, which holds that once a judicial matter is resolved, the parties cannot relitigate the same issue. Res judicata applies as much to quasi-judicial decisions as to judicial decisions. That said, if an application is modified substantially, the relevant ordinance provisions change, or material conditions at the site change, a second application that presents new issues may be heard as an entirely new proceeding.[36]

---

34. G.S. 132-3 & G.S. 121-5.
35. Little v. City of Raleigh, 195 N.C. 793, 143 S.E. 827 (1928).
36. *In re* Broughton Estate, 210 N.C. 62, 185 S.E. 434 (1936).

# Chapter 6
# **Variances**

Boards of adjustment are authorized to vary the standards of a development regulation ordinance when the ordinance creates an unnecessary hardship for an owner. State law defines the "unnecessary hardship" standard, and the applicant for a variance must show that she or he meets it.

## **Applicability**

Typically, everyone must comply with the general rules. All property owners share the necessary hardships of reasonable regulation. In certain limited circumstances, however, individual property owners need relief from unnecessary hardship resulting from regulation.

The General Statutes direct boards of adjustment to vary the provisions of the zoning ordinance if its strict application is found to create unnecessary hardship.[1] Before obtaining a variance, though, the applicant must show that

1. the unnecessary hardship results from the strict application of the ordinance;
2. the unnecessary hardship results from conditions that are peculiar to the applicant's property;
3. the unnecessary hardship is not a self-created hardship;
4. the requested variance is consistent with the spirit, purpose, and intent of the ordinance such that public safety is secured and substantial justice is achieved.

Notably the statute prohibits any use variance. For example, if commercial land uses are prohibited for a site, the board cannot grant a variance to allow a retail store. If the owner desires to undertake a prohibited use, a rezoning or zoning text amendment is required, not a variance.

---

1. G.S. 160A-388(d).

It is unclear if, and how much, the local ordinance may clarify the variance standards. State law requires that if a property owner meets the basic standards, the board must issue the variance. State law also provides that the board of adjustment may vary zoning regulations "in harmony with their general purpose and intent *and in accordance with general or specific rules.*"[2] It may be permissible therefore for the local ordinance to give some additional guiding rules for the state-mandated variance standards, provided that guidance is consistent with the state standards.

Not just zoning ordinances, but any other ordinance that regulates land use or development may also provide for variances. Subdivision ordinances, stormwater and erosion control ordinances, and other development-related ordinances may provide for variances and use the same standards and process as those in zoning variances.[3]

In addition to providing for variances, zoning and other development ordinances may provide for other types of modifications, such as administrative modifications. Moreover, certain related regulations have specific variance or modification standards. The Model Flood Damage Prevention Ordinance, for example, includes a standard for variances to that ordinance.

The following discussion walks through each of the standards that the applicant must meet for a zoning variance.

## Unnecessary Hardship Resulting from Strict Application

As noted above, unnecessary hardship must result from the strict application of the ordinance. All regulation involves some level of necessary hardship and inconvenience shared by the entire community. To apply for a variance, an applicant must show that the hardship is unnecessary.

There is no simple answer to calculating what constitutes unnecessary hardship—it is determined on a case-by-case basis. The board of adjustment holds a quasi-judicial hearing, considers the evidence presented, and uses its judgment to make the determination. The hardship must be more than a mere inconvenience to the property owner. So, for example, a simple preference for a lenient height restriction is not enough, nor is it enough for

---

2. G.S. 160A-381(b1) (emphasis added).
3. G.S. 160A-388(d).

an applicant to claim that complying with the development will cost more. The applicant must show that the nature of the hardship is far greater for the applicant than for others subject to the same restriction.

Under prior law, some jurisdictions required that an applicant must show that no reasonable use of the property was available without a variance. That standard is no longer allowed, however.[4] A property owner may establish an unnecessary hardship even if the owner would still have some reasonable use of the property without the variance.

## Peculiar to the Property

The unnecessary hardship must be peculiar to the property, not general to the neighborhood or public. Such peculiar characteristics might arise, for example, from location of the property, size or shape of the lot, or topography or other natural features on the site.

A variance is not the appropriate remedy for a condition or hardship that is shared by the neighborhood or the public as a whole. Such conditions are either appropriate to general regulations or should be addressed through an ordinance amendment. So, for example, think about an older neighborhood in town where all of the lots are small and narrow. Given the applicable side-yard setback, no owner is able to add a modern detached garage. The burden is shared by the neighborhood; it is not unique to a particular property. If setbacks are to be relaxed, that should be accomplished through an amendment to the ordinance applicable to all, not through case-by-case variances.

Hardship must be peculiar to the *property*, not the *property owner*. Hardships resulting from personal circumstances may not be the basis for granting a variance. Bringing an elderly parent to live with the family, for example, is a change in personal circumstance, not a condition peculiar to the property. A variance decision must not be based on the applicant's ability to cover the cost of the hardship. That the applicant owns property nearby is irrelevant to the consideration of whether the circumstances of this particular property warrant a variance.[5]

---

4. G.S. 160A-388(d)(1).

5. Williams v. N.C. Dep't of Envtl. & Natural Res., 144 N.C. App. 479, 548 S.E. 2d 793 (2001).

Note that federal law requires local governments to make reasonable accommodation for persons with disabilities.[6] The variance standard set by state law is inappropriate for handling such modifications, so local governments should establish another form of administrative relief to provide reasonable accommodation, such as allowing a waiver from the rules upon showing that a reasonable accommodation is necessary.

## Hardship Not Self-Created

The hardship must not result from actions taken by the applicant or property owner. So for example, if a property owner sells part of a lot (moving the setback lines and reducing buildable area), the owner cannot then seek a variance for building into the setback. Similarly, where an owner fails to comply with zoning and building permits and places foundation footings in the setback, the hardship is self-created. No variance is allowed.

What if the owner relied in good faith on seemingly valid surveys and obtained building permits but later discovered that the survey was incorrect or the permits were improperly granted? Can the owner seek a variance? Probably so. North Carolina courts have held that hardships resulting from such good faith reliance on surveys and permits are eligible for a variance.[7]

The General Statutes include an important provision that applies to self-created hardship: "The act of purchasing property with knowledge that circumstances exist that may justify the granting of a variance shall not be regarded as a self-created hardship."[8] So, if the original owner had a legitimate case for a variance, a purchaser buying the lot from the original owner would have the same legal position as the original owner. The new owner may seek a variance.

Restrictive covenants and other legal limitations *may* be a factor in determining hardship. Consider a property that has limited development ability due to a privately imposed covenant for a street setback and a publicly imposed stream setback. Can the owner seek a variance from the public stream setback? In one particular case, the North Carolina Supreme Court

---

6. Fair Housing Act, 42 U.S.C. § 3604(f)(3) (2017).

7. Turik v. Town of Surf City, 182 N.C. App. 427, 434, 642 S.E.2d 251, 255 (2007).

8. G.S. 160A-388(d)(3).

ruled that the board of adjustment should consider physical *and* legal conditions of the property, including restrictive covenants.[9]

To reiterate, covenants and other legal limitations *may* be a factor. In the case mentioned above, the covenants were in place prior to adoption of the stream setback, the decision was based on the local ordinance, and the decision pre-dated the statutory variance standards. A self-imposed legal limitation that was created after a zoning ordinance limitation became effective—for example, an easement across a property that limits buildable area—may be viewed as a self-imposed hardship, and no variance should be granted.

## Purpose, Safety, and Justice

In addition to the standards for unnecessary hardship, the General Statutes require an applicant to show that the variance being requested "is consistent with the spirit, purpose, and intent of the ordinance, such that public safety is secured, and substantial justice is achieved."[10]

Oftentimes the ordinance will include purpose and intent language. Such language should guide the consideration of the variance. Where an ordinance expresses a clear intent, a variance cannot subvert that intent.

In one court case, an applicant was seeking a variance to allow an additional sign at a secondary entrance. The North Carolina Court of Appeals looked to the purpose language of the ordinance and found that it sought to provide "adequate and effective signage," "prevent driver confusion," and "allow for flexibility to meet individual needs for business identification." The purpose, the court found, allowed for the flexibility that the applicant sought in the variance.[11]

Beyond the purpose of the ordinance, the applicant also must show that the variance does not harm public safety and achieves substantial justice. Even if an applicant meets the standard for unnecessary hardship, a variance may be denied for public safety concerns.

---

9. Chapel Hill Title & Abstract Co., Inc. v. Town of Chapel Hill, 362 N.C. 649, 653, 669 S.E.2d 286, 288 (2008).

10. G.S. 160A-388(d)(4).

11. Premier Plastic Surgery Ctr., PLLC v. Bd. of Adjustment for Town of Matthews, 213 N.C. App. 364, 369, 713 S.E.2d 511, 515 (2011).

As described above, the General Statutes also require the applicant to show that through the variance, "substantial justice is achieved." Determining *substantial justice* is much like determining *unnecessary hardship*—it requires judgment and is decided on a case-by-case basis.

## No Use Variance

As an extension of the requirement that any variance be consistent with the purpose of the ordinance, use variances are not permitted. The North Carolina Supreme Court long ago noted that the board of adjustment "cannot disregard the provisions of the statute or its regulations. It can merely 'vary' them to prevent injustice when the strict letter of the provisions would work 'unnecessary hardship.'" [12] The court found that a board cannot grant variances for use restrictions, and that rule is now written into state law. [13]

Note that some uses are distinguished by density and intensity. If only single-family residences are permitted in a district, for example, a variance cannot permit a duplex. [14]

## Process

In addition to the general provisions applicable to all quasi-judicial decisions discussed in previous chapters, several process-related matters should be kept in mind whenever variance requests are considered.

**Evidence.** A variance decision is handled by the assigned board, typically the board of adjustment, through a quasi-judicial hearing. The applicant bears the burden of bringing forth competent, relevant, and substantial evidence to show why the situation meets the standards for a variance. Similarly, any opponents may bring evidence as to why the applicant fails to meet the standards.

**Conditions.** The board may impose conditions on a variance approval as long as those conditions reasonably relate to the variance. If a variance

---

12. Lee v. Bd. of Adjustment of City of Rocky Mount, 226 N.C. 107, 111, 37 S.E.2d 128, 132 (1946).
13. G.S. 160A-388(d).
14. Sherrill v. Town of Wrightsville Beach, 76 N.C. App. 646, 334 S.E.2d 103 (1985).

allows construction in the setback, for example, the board might require additional landscaping or fencing to mitigate the impact on neighbors.

**Motion and vote.** As discussed in Chapter 5, state law requires a four-fifths majority of the board to grant a variance. This means that the *votes for* divided by the *total number of board members* must be equal to or greater than 0.8. For purposes of calculating the vote for quasi-judicial decisions, vacant positions and members recused from participating are not included as members of the board unless a qualified alternate is available to take their place.

The supermajority requirement can create quirky situations. As shown below, a board may have a majority (a *simple* majority) in favor of granting the variance, but without the four-fifths majority the variance fails. If a board adopts findings by a simple majority, then the findings may be contrary to the ultimate decision that is adopted by a four-fifths majority. Following are a few options to help avoid such scenarios from occurring:

- It is a useful and usual practice for boards to phrase motions regarding a variance in the affirmative (to approve), even if board members intend to deny the variance. That way the supermajority calculation is clear.
- It is not necessary to make an additional motion to deny a variance if a motion to approve fails to get the required four-fifths majority, as the variance is denied by virtue of the motion to approve failing to get the supermajority vote. Or, alternatively, a motion to deny a variance needs only a simple majority.
- Members voting in the minority will in some cases need to outline findings of fact. If a majority—but not a supermajority—support the variance, the minority members should outline the evidence and considerations that were critical to their decision to oppose the variance.

## CALCULATING A VARIANCE VOTE

The board of adjustment heard a variance case and now must vote. It is a seven-member board with no vacancy, no absences, and no recusals. Five members vote in favor of granting the variance. Two vote against. The calculation looks like the following:

(5 votes for variance) / (7 total members of board) = 0.714.
0.714 is less than 0.8, so the variance fails.

Alternatively, suppose that the same seven-member board is voting, but two members of the board are absent this week and one member is recused due to a conflict of interest. Four board members are present and voting. They vote unanimously to approve the variance (4–0 in favor of granting). It may seem as if the variance should be granted—the vote is unanimous after all—but careful calculation is needed. The recusal does not count toward the *total members of the board*, but the absences do still count toward the *total members of the board*. For the calculation there are six (6) members of the board. The calculation looks as follows:

(4 votes for variance) / (6 total members of the board) = 0.66.
0.66 is less than 0.8, so the variance fails.

Having alternate members of the board to serve when regular members are absent or have conflicts can help avoid this situation.

# Chapter 7
# Special Use Permits

Special use permits are a valuable and useful zoning tool. They allow a landowner a broader range of potential uses of his or her property, but do so in a way that assures that development does not harm the neighbors or surrounding community.

Special use permits require a fair amount of work for everyone involved. The applicant must produce convincing evidence that the project under consideration has been designed to meet ordinance standards. The neighbors must base any objections on reliable evidence that the standards would not be met. The board must conduct an evidentiary hearing and apply the determined facts to the standards in the ordinance, all of which should be reflected in a written decision.

Properly done, this provides a useful degree of flexibility in the ordinance. It lets the landowner and the neighbors know what standards must be met before such a use can be permitted on a site. It requires a thorough, fair and unbiased review of each application.

This tool should not be used for routine, objective decisions, nor as a vehicle to decide broadly what should be allowed or to figure out whether a particular type of land use or project would generally be good for the community. In the right circumstances, though, it allows useful flexibility and careful review of individual applications to the benefit of the landowner, the neighbors, and the community.

## Special Use Permits Defined

Zoning ordinances divide a jurisdiction's territory into various zoning districts. Each district has a list of permitted land uses along with the development standards that go with them. If the use is permitted and meets objective standards, such as height limits and setbacks, the project is automatically approved by the staff. If not, the project is denied.

A local government may want to add flexibility to this set of zoning regulations. Rather than put everything into a "yes" or "no" category based on entirely objective standards, the local government may want to include a few "maybes" in the ordinance. For example, a city might conclude that small apartment projects would potentially be acceptable within a particular residential zoning district but not everywhere in the district and not in all circumstances. Thus, before allowing any small apartment to be built in this district, the city wants to undertake a careful, public review of each application to be sure that the project site and design fit within the neighborhood. The special use permit is the zoning ordinance tool that allows for this kind of flexibility.

Authority to have special use permits has always been a part of zoning. Originally referred to as "special exceptions," they are now called "special use permits" or "conditional use permits."[1] Whatever name is given to them, special exceptions, special use permits, and conditional use permits are legally the same thing: a way to allow a particular land use in a zoning district only upon a finding that specified standards will be met. The process and standards for decisions are the same no matter which board makes the decision. While individual zoning ordinances may use other names for these tools, for the sake of convenience, the rest of this chapter will refer to them as "special use permits."

Special use permits must be explicitly authorized by the zoning ordinance. A landowner is allowed to apply for only those special use permits specifically listed in the ordinance. The ordinance must specify which uses may be allowed as a special use, in what zoning districts they are allowed, and what standards they must meet.

A zoning ordinance does not have to include special use permits. If a city or county elects not to use this tool, there is no requirement that special use permits be authorized in its zoning ordinance. However, most North Carolina zoning ordinances do include special use permits. School of Government surveys indicate that special use permits are included in more than 90 percent of North Carolina zoning regulations.

When a special use permit application is considered, the decision-making board must follow all of the quasi-judicial procedures that have been described in this book.

---

1. G.S. 153A-340(c1); G.S. 160A-381(c), -388(c).

In some situations, local government officials may determine that a formal evidentiary hearing with due process protections is inappropriate. They may prefer a legislative process, with greater discretion and a more informal decision-making process. Individualized site-specific conditions cannot be imposed in a rezoning to a conventional zoning district, as all of the standards must be applied uniformly throughout the district. In the past the only way an elected board could add the flexibility to consider tailored, site-specific conditions was through a special use permit review. However, since 2001 North Carolina case law has allowed conditional zoning,[2] and in 2005 the General Statutes were amended to authorize purely legislative conditional zoning, which allows elected officials to apply site-specific conditions in a rezoning.

Since conditional zoning is a highly discretionary legislative decision, it provides less certainty and predictability than a quasi-judicial special use permit review. But because it is a less formal process allowing for greater discretion, conditional zoning has proven to be popular with many local governments. This particularly holds true when the decision is assigned to the elected governing board. A number of local governments that want to assign these development reviews to their elected boards have opted to shift from a special use permit to conditional zoning. This is a prudent step, as it avoids the very real risk that elected officials who are accustomed to a legislative process might inappropriately follow legislative procedures when making a quasi-judicial decision on a special use permit application.

## Who Decides a Special Use Permit
### Options for the Decision-Making Board

If a zoning ordinance authorizes special use permits, state law gives cities and counties three choices to decide who makes the decisions on them, as follows:

1. the governing board,
2. the planning board, or
3. the board of adjustment.

---

2. Massey v. City of Charlotte, 145 N.C. App. 345, 550 S.E.2d 838, *review denied*, 354 N.C. 219, 554 S.E.2d 342 (2001); Summers v. City of Charlotte, 149 N.C. App. 509, 562 S.E.2d 18, *review denied*, 355 N.C. 758, 566 S.E.2d 482 (2002).

Special use permit decisions may not be assigned to local government staff. Staff plays an important role in analyzing applications, but decision-making must be assigned to one of the boards noted above. Also, the choice of the assignment must be made in the ordinance itself and cannot be varied on a case-by-case basis.

In North Carolina, special use permit decisions are most commonly assigned to the governing board. A substantial number of cities and counties also send at least some types of special use permits to their board of adjustment. Only a few jurisdictions assign final decisions on these to the planning board.

When the city council or the board of county commissioners takes on this responsibility, it is critical that the elected board members fully understand that in hearing a special use permit application they are making a judicial-like decision. They must follow the same quasi-judicial procedures that apply to a board of adjustment and not treat these as if they were legislative rezoning decisions. To avoid confusion by applicants, board members, and the public regarding the type of process that must be observed, an increasing number of jurisdictions have taken the step of assigning all quasi-judicial decisions for development regulations to the board of adjustment, with all advisory decisions going to the planning board and all legislative decisions to the governing board. This is not required by law but is a judicious step that should be seriously considered.

It is possible to assign some of the decisions to one board and others to a different board. For example, large, complex special use permits may be assigned to the city council or board of county commissioners while more routine cases are assigned to the board of adjustment. This is permissible if the ordinance itself clearly defines which applications go to which board for a decision. The same hearing and decision-making process must be followed by any board making special use permit decisions.

What should a local government consider when assigning decision-making responsibility for special use permits?

A key issue is whether the board will have adequate time to address the applications received. Each special use permit application requires an evidentiary hearing. These typically take thirty to sixty minutes to conduct. While a simple project may go more quickly, it is not unusual for a complicated or highly contested application to have a hearing that runs several hours or even several days. The city or county will need to consider how many applications they expect to receive and be sure that the board deciding special use permits has enough time to adequately deal with them. The experience, expertise, and judgment that a decision-making board must exercise also are important considerations.

### Advisory Review

It is fairly common in North Carolina for special use permit applications to get an informal review by an advisory board before being presented to the decision-making board.

This practice, while popular, poses some significant potential legal concerns. For one, only the evidence properly presented to the decision-making board and made a part of the hearing record can be considered in determining a special use permit application. Evidence that is presented only to the advisory board must not be considered. Similarly, the comment of the advisory board may identify areas and topics that the decision-making board will want to look at carefully, but the recommendation itself is unlikely to constitute admissible evidence that can be used in the decision.

That said, advisory review remains popular with many local governments. It allows for a less formal "dry-run" that can help the applicant and the applicant's neighbors identify issues of concern and assess where additional witnesses, expert testimony, or documentary evidence need to be gathered prior to the formal evidentiary hearing. It also often serves as a forum in which potential conditions on the permit can be identified and discussed.

### Standards Set by Ordinance

The zoning ordinance must include the standards to be applied in deciding special use permits. While the standards can be general in nature and involve the exercise of some judgment, they must be sufficient to guide the applicant, neighbors, decision-making board, and a reviewing court.

Special use permits are not legislative decisions. Therefore, providing only an extremely general standard, such as that the project must be in the public interest, is not sufficient.[3] Similarly, if the only standard for approval

---

3. Jackson v. Guilford Cty. Bd. of Adjustment, 275 N.C. 155, 166 S.E.2d 78 (1969).

is that the permit be consistent with the purpose and intent of the zoning ordinance, or that it be consistent with the goals and objectives of the plan, that also is insufficient.[4] A very general standard grants such broad discretion as to be an unlawful delegation of legislative authority.


## Typical Standards

North Carolina courts have approved a set of four general standards that provide sufficient guidance to decision-making boards.[5] These are now the most commonly used standards for special use permits in the state. They are that the project

1. does not materially endanger public health or safety;
2. will not substantially injure the value of adjoining property or, if so, is a public necessity;
3. will be in harmony with or compatible with its neighbors and generally consistent with the comprehensive plan; and
4. will meet all required conditions and specifications.

In addition to the above *general* standards that are applied to all special uses, many local governments set *specific* standards for some or all of the individual types of uses as laid out in the individual zoning ordinance. Unlike for variances, where one standard set by state law is applied uniformly across the state, special use permit standards are set by each individual zoning ordinance.

For example, more detailed standards may be included for day care centers, telecommunication towers, multifamily housing, and so on. Typically these additional standards address such issues as buffers, landscaping, noise limits, parking, or other issues peculiar to the specific land use involved. Most ordinances require that a proposed project meet all of the general standards as well as the more specific standards related to some special uses.

---

4. Keiger v. Bd. of Adjustment, 278 N.C. 17, 178 S.E.2d 616 (1971).

5. Kenan v. Bd. of Adjustment, 13 N.C. App. 688, 692–93, 187 S.E.2d 496, 499, *review denied*, 281 N.C. 314, 188 S.E.2d 897 (1972).

## In Harmony and Compatible with Neighborhood

The fact that a land use is included as a potential special use within a particular zoning district is a legislative finding that it is at least in general harmony with the other permitted uses within that zoning district.[6] Thus opponents may not simply object to the use in general and expect it to be denied.

If the board finds that a use is not in harmony or compatible with the neighborhood, specific evidence must be submitted as to why that is so for this particular application. For example, the height, bulk, scale, design, or appearance of a specific proposed project may be judged to be incompatible with the area where it is proposed. In that case, the board must identify evidence laying out the specific ways in which the proposal is incompatible and not simply a generalized objection to the use.

## No Significant Adverse Impacts on Property Values

Preservation of a community's property values has long been held to be a legitimate objective of development regulations and is a near-universal standard for special use permits. Assessing the impacts of a proposed project on neighboring property values is often the key issue in contentious special use permit applications.

Establishing whether a proposed project will or will not harm property values is often a difficult task. North Carolina local governments report the potential impact on property values as being the single most difficult standard for their boards to apply.[7] Another concern is that the way in which the standard is phrased in the ordinance can have significant consequences on who has the burden of producing evidence on this point. Many ordinances state that a special use permit may be granted absent a finding that the use will cause significant adverse impacts on neighboring property values. This places the burden on opponents to show how property values will be harmed. Absent the presentation of substantial evidence of harm, the standard is presumed met. Other ordinances state that the applicant must show that the permit will *not* cause harm to neighboring property values. If this point is contested by permit opponents, the applicant must

---

6. Harts Book Stores v. City of Raleigh, 53 N.C. App. 753, 281 S.E.2d 761 (1981).

7. David W. Owens, Special Use Permits in North Carolina Zoning 14 (School of Government Special Series No. 22, Apr. 2007).

produce substantial evidence that the use will not have the asserted harmful impacts. In some settings this can be quite challenging.

Testimony that shows specific adverse impacts—noise, traffic, environmental harm, and the like—can provide a foundation for findings of fact regarding impacts on property values. Witnesses, however, must not only establish that the negative impacts will occur; they also must show the ways in which those impacts will in fact hurt neighboring property values.

Special care is needed when moving beyond testimony about facts to the consideration of opinions about the impact of those facts on property values. The General Statutes specifically limit the use of opinion testimony to address property value impacts.[8] The board cannot base a finding about property value impacts on opinion testimony unless it is offered by a qualified expert witness who has conducted a formal study of the potential impacts. For example, a qualified real estate appraiser who has conducted a study involving appropriate comparable properties and projects can offer a professional opinion as to whether the project will affect property values, and the board can rely on that opinion in making its decision. But a nonexpert witness simply saying "I believe this will hurt my property values" cannot in and of itself be the basis for a finding that the project would have an adverse impact on neighboring property values.

## Public Safety

Generalized fears about crime, traffic, or public safety are inadequate grounds to deny a special use permit.[9] For objections of this nature, the evidence needs to show why this particular use at the specified site has a reasonable likelihood of causing such adverse impacts. For example, a witness could testify about traffic accidents he or she has seen at the site, or a technical traffic impact study could be presented at the hearing. The board must have specific, reliable, factual testimony about the impacts of this project at this site, not broad generalizations and speculation.

As with property value impacts, the General Statutes specifically limit the use of opinion testimony about the impact of traffic on public safety.[10] The board cannot rely upon opinion testimony about traffic safety unless

---

8. G.S. 160A-393(k)(3).

9. Sun Suites Holdings, LLC v. Town of Garner, 139 N.C. App. 269, 533 S.E.2d 525, *review denied*, 353 N.C. 470, 666 S.E.2d 397 (2000).

10. G.S. 160A-393(k)(3).

it is offered by a qualified expert witness who has conducted a formal study of the potential impacts of the special use being requested. Non-expert witnesses also can offer factual testimony about traffic. For example, a non-expert witness may testify about traffic accidents he has seen at the site, the amount of traffic she has experienced there, or the condition of the roadway. These are all observed facts. But a witness who wants to offer an opinion on future traffic impacts needs to be a properly qualified expert witness and offer testimony that is based on a proper foundation. The board can rely on the facts presented by a non-expert witness to reach its conclusions about traffic safety impacts, but the board cannot base its conclusions on the opinions offered by a non-expert on this issue.

## Burden

As with other quasi-judicial decisions, the burden of providing evidence to show that the standards for a special use permit will be met falls initially on the applicant. If the applicant meets that burden by producing uncontroverted evidence that the standards are met, the special use permit must be granted.[11] If the applicant does not produce sufficient evidence to show that the standards will be met, the application must be denied.[12] Typically, the special use permit application form asks the applicant to supply the information needed to establish compliance with the standards. This form, along with any supporting documents, is submitted and made a part of the hearing record. The applicant also typically testifies or presents evidence at the hearing to show that each standard will be met.

Once the applicant has produced evidence to show that the standards will be met, the burden shifts to the opponents. If the opponents fail to produce sufficient evidence to show that the standards will not be met, the permit must be issued.

There is an important qualification to these general rules that applies to special use permits. For a very general permit standard, such as "the project will not harm the public health, safety, or welfare," the burden generally rests with the challenger to show that the standard will not be met.[13] The

---

11. Howard v. City of Kinston, 148 N.C. App. 238, 558 S.E.2d 221 (2002).
12. Signorelli v. Town of Highlands, 93 N.C. App. 704, 379 S.E.2d 55 (1989).
13. Woodhouse v. Bd. of Comm'rs, 299 N.C. 211, 219, 261 S.E.2d 882, 887–88 (1980).

same is true to a degree with the harmonious and compatible use requirement in that a use is generally considered harmonious absent a showing of
specific reasons why a particular application would be inharmonious. However, it is important to consider the exact language of the ordinance. For
example, many ordinances say a special use permit will be denied if it will
harm the public health, safety, or welfare; this leaves the burden on project
opponents to produce a showing of harm to these interests. Alternatively,
the ordinance could say the applicant must show that the project will not
harm public safety; this effectively places the burden on the applicant to
show that any safety issue raised is not sufficient to violate the standard.[14]
As with other issues, if there is conflicting evidence about whether these
general standards will be met, the board resolves what it believes the facts
to be and decides on the permit accordingly.

In most cities and counties the administrative staff also submits a report
on the application. This may include staff analysis, background information,
and, in some jurisdictions, a recommendation about the decision. The staff
report should be made a part of the hearing record, and the staff person
who prepared it should be available as a witness to present the report and
answer any questions about it.

## Approval and Conditions

The board may approve the application or deny it. The General Statutes
allow "reasonable and appropriate conditions and safeguards" on any special use permit.[15] For example, the board may approve a special use permit
but add a condition, such as specifying that a vegetated buffer is needed
to prevent harm to neighboring property values or adjusting the height or
setback of buildings to make them fit within the neighborhood.

There are several important limitations on the conditions that can be
imposed. First, any mandated exaction of land, construction, or payment of
fees must have specific statutory authorization. Second, only the standards
for approval of the permit set out in the ordinance can be considered, so
any conditions need to be reasonably related to bringing the project into

---

14. Mann Media, Inc. v. Randolph Cty. Planning Bd., 356 N.C. 1, 565 S.E.2d 9 (2002).
15. G.S. 160A-381(c), -388(c).

compliance with those standards. Third, since this is a quasi-judicial decision, there must be competent, material, and substantial evidence in the hearing record that justifies the need for the condition.

# Chapter 8
# Certificates of Appropriateness

State law allows cities and counties to establish local historic districts and historic landmarks. After the local designation, property owners must request and obtain a certificate of appropriateness (COA) from the preservation commission to make changes to their property. The preservation commission[1] reviews those requests to determine if the requested change is incongruous with the character of the district or landmark. Because judgment is required to make a COA decision, it is a quasi-judicial decision that should follow the standard procedural requirements for all quasi-judicial decisions.

## Authority

Historic districts and landmarks are established by cities and counties in areas with properties that are deemed to have special significance in terms of history, architecture, and/or culture.[2] Property owners must secure a COA for any construction, alteration, moving, or demolition of any exterior feature of a designated property. The preservation ordinance may allow for administrative approval of minor works based on detailed standards adopted by the preservation commission. Minor works subject to administrative approval might include such items as fence type or height, in-kind material replacement, and minor changes to the rear of the property not visible from the front. Minor works may be approved by staff, but any denial must still be made by the commission.

---

1. The local historic preservation commission may be composed in a variety of ways—a landmark commission, a districts commission, a planning board, and otherwise. The term "preservation commission" is used interchangeably here for all allowed commission varieties operating under G.S. 160A-400. G.S. 160A-400.7.

2. G.S. 160A-400.1–.15.

## Quasi-Judicial Procedures Apply

The preservation commission's authority is to prevent changes and new development that "would be incongruous with the special character of the landmark or district."[3] That standard—the incongruity standard—requires the judgment of the board. In other words, it is a quasi-judicial standard. As such, parties involved in a COA decision have rights to the basic elements of a fair trial, and the preservation commission must follow quasi-judicial procedures.

A few basic procedural elements are outlined in the General Statutes.[4] The preservation commission

- "shall take such steps as may be reasonably required in the ordinance and/or rules of procedure to inform the owners of any property likely to be materially affected by the application";
- "shall give the applicant and such owners an opportunity to be heard";
- "may hold a public hearing concerning the application";
- shall review and act upon all applications "within a reasonable time, not to exceed 180 days from the date the application for a certificate of appropriateness is filed."

An appeal of a COA decision to the board of adjustment "(i) may be taken by any aggrieved party, (ii) shall be taken within times prescribed by the preservation commission by general rule, and (iii) shall be in the nature of certiorari."[5] Appeals are discussed in greater detail below.

Because the incongruity standard is a quasi-judicial standard, preservation commissions should follow additional procedural standards to protect the due process rights of the parties. As discussed in Chapter 4, the applicable quasi-judicial procedural requirements include

- notice of the hearing mailed to the property owner, applicant, and the owners of abutting parcels as well as a sign posted on the site;
- impartial decision-makers, free from bias, conflicts of interest and undisclosed ex parte communications;

---

3. G.S. 160A-400.9(a).
4. G.S. 160A-400.9(c) & (d).
5. G.S. 160A-400.9(e).

- an evidentiary hearing with witnesses offering sworn testimony (not mere opinion);
- opinion testimony limited to qualified experts;
- the right of a party to be heard and to cross-examine witnesses;
- a simple majority vote for a decision;
- a decision
  - in a reasonable time,
  - supported by competent, material, substantial evidence in the record,
  - determining contested facts and applying applicable standards;
- notice of the decision by written decision document delivered to the applicant and other requesting parties by personal delivery, email, or first-class mail;
- the right of a party to appeal.

As a board making a quasi-judicial decision, the preservation commission apparently is required to follow these stricter procedural requirements. Regardless, it is prudent to follow them.

## COA Standards and Decisions
### Incongruity as a Contextual Standard

The North Carolina Supreme Court explains the incongruity standard to be "a contextual standard."[6]

A contextual standard is one which derives its meaning from the objectively determinable, interrelated conditions and characteristics of the subject to which the standard is to be applied. In this instance the standard of "incongruity" must derive its meaning, if any, from the total physical environment of the Historic District. That is to say, the conditions and characteristics of the Historic District's physical environment must be sufficiently distinctive and identifiable to provide reasonable guidance to the Historic District Commission in applying the "incongruity" standard.[7]

---

6. A-S-P Assocs. v. City of Raleigh, 298 N.C. 207, 222, 258 S.E.2d 444, 454 (1979).
7. *Id.* (citation omitted).

The character of the district or landmark is not left to speculation or guesswork. It is not conjured up at the time of COA review. State law requires the local government to distill and clarify the character and context of the historic district or landmark at the time of designation and to establish principles and guidelines for COAs.

Before the local governing board may establish a historic district, the local government must draft and submit to the State Historic Preservation Officer (SHPO) an "investigation and report describing the significance of the buildings, structures, features, sites or surroundings included in any such proposed district, and a description of the boundaries of such district."[8] The SHPO, in turn, provides a written analysis and recommendations regarding the proposed designation within thirty days of submittal. The local government must draft and submit to the SHPO a similar document for historic landmarks, and the SHPO has a similar opportunity to respond. In addition, the ordinance designating the landmark "shall describe each property designated in the ordinance, the name or names of the owner or owners of the property, those elements of the property that are integral to its historical, architectural, or prehistorical value, including the land area of the property so designated."[9]

Separately the preservation commission must "prepare and adopt principles and guidelines . . . for new construction, alterations, additions, moving and demolition."[10] Some communities incorporate and use the Secretary of the Interior's Standards for the Treatment of Historic Properties[11] as well as more detailed and illustrated design guidelines tailored to the historic context of locally designated areas.

In other words, *prior* to designating areas as local historic districts and/or landmarks and the preservation commission engaging in COA review, the local government must investigate and report on the elements justifying the designation of a historic district and/or landmark and establish clear design principles and guidelines to guide the commission in determining if a change is incongruous with the district.

---

8. G.S. 160A-400.4.

9. G.S. 160A-400.5.

10. G.S. 160A-400.9.

11. Available from Technical Preservation Services, National Park Service, U.S. Department of the Interior, at www.nps.gov/tps/standards.htm.

## Evidence

As with any quasi-judicial decision, a decision on a COA must be based on competent, relevant, substantial evidence in the record. The record is composed of the application, any staff analysis or reports, testimony and documents presented at the evidentiary hearing, and other related documents.

State law specifically highlights the role and usefulness of site visits and expert opinion in the decision-making process. "As part of its review procedure, the commission may view the premises and seek the advice of the Division of Archives and History or such other expert advice as it may deem necessary under the circumstances."[12] Advice from the state or other experts is advisory; the preservation commission is not bound by those opinions. As discussed in Chapter 3, commissioners should avoid ex parte communications during site visits and should disclose site visits at the evidentiary hearing.

## Limited Discretion

The incongruity standard does not grant the preservation commission "untrammeled authority to compel individual property owners in the Historic District to comply with whatever arbitrary or subjective views the members of the Commission might have as to how property in the district should be maintained or developed."[13] A decision to grant or deny a COA must be framed within the character of the district and based on evidence in the record. Otherwise, that decision is arbitrary and cannot stand.

Moreover, incongruity must be based on "the total physical environment of the Historic District." The commission cannot cherry pick features of certain properties from elsewhere in the district to determine incongruity.[14]

---

12. G.S. 160A-400.9(d); the former Division of Archives and History is now the Office of Archives and History, N.C. Department of Natural and Cultural Resources.

13. *A-S-P Associates*, 298 N.C. at 221, 258 S.E.2d at 453 (quoting plaintiff's argument).

14. Sanchez v. Town of Beaufort, 211 N.C. App. 574, 580–81, 710 S.E.2d 350, 354–55 (2011).

## CLEARLY ARBITRARY

North Carolina courts have ruled that when a preservation commission decision departs from the framework of historic standards and guidelines, that decision is arbitrary and will not stand. In *Sanchez v. Town of Beaufort*, for example, the court disapprovingly noted that the "height requirement was not reached on the basis of any particular determining principle. Rather, each [commission] member reached what he or she considered an appropriate height based on their own personal preferences."*

The court of appeals quoted commissioners discussing the height requirement in loose terms, unmoored from standards. One commissioner argued that the project could be redesigned to reduce five feet in height. When the chair asked for the basis for the five feet, the commissioner offered

> Well five feet (5') would be if you had a . . . . This is his determination, with a ten foot (10') ceiling downstairs, and a nine foot (9') ceiling upstairs, if you had eight foot (8') ceilings, that's three feet (3'). . . . And then, if the duct work was to be relocated, that's two more feet. So that would be five feet (5') without a lot of material changes. *Now it could be a different number, but I'm just throwing that out.***

Another commissioner made his own calculations for how the project could be redesigned. A third commissioner stated simply that "twenty five feet (25') is a reasonable height." When the commission voted on the height limit one commissioner "explicitly admitted that none of the [commission] guidelines were used to determine that height."

The court was clear: "Since the twenty-four foot height requirement was established by each member of the [commission] without the use of any determining principle from the BHPC guidelines, it was clearly arbitrary."***

* *Sanchez v. Town of Beaufort*, 211 N.C. App. 574, 581, 710 S.E.2d 350, 355 (2011).
** *Id*. (emphasis added by court).
*** *Id*. at 582, 710 S.E.2d at 355.

## Conditions

A preservation commission may issue a COA subject to reasonable conditions necessary to ensure that the proposed development will not be incongruous with the character of the district.[15] Conditions must be specific and set forth in the written COA.

## Appeals

State law provides that a decision on a COA may be appealed to the board of adjustment. Such appeals may be made by an aggrieved party (a party with standing in the case). Appeals must be made within the time prescribed by the preservation commission's rules (commonly thirty days). The board of adjustment's decision, in turn, can be appealed to superior court.[16]

Appeals of COA decisions are "in the nature of certiorari," which is different from the nature of other hearings the board of adjustment holds. For an appeal in the nature of certiorari, the board of adjustment acts like a superior court when it reviews a board of adjustment decision on a variance.[17] Below are some guidelines for how the board of adjustment reviews an appeal of a COA decision from the preservation commission.

**On the record.** The appeal is based on the record from below. The board of adjustment does not take in new evidence on the factual questions of the case. The board of adjustment does not make its own independent decision about whether or not to grant the COA. Rather, the board of adjustment must determine if there is competent, relevant, and substantial evidence in the record to support the decision that the preservation commission made. To reiterate, the board of adjustment does not ask, "Would we choose to approve or deny?" The board of adjustment asks, "Is there evidence in the record to support the preservation commission's decision (to approve or deny)?"

**Questions of law.** A party may appeal a preservation commission decision based on a question of law. For example, the applicant may challenge the preservation commission's interpretation of the ordinance. The board

---

15. G.S. 160A-400.9(a).
16. G.S. 160A-400.9.
17. G.S. 160A-393.

of adjustment may hear legal arguments (not new factual testimony) from the parties and make its own decision about the correct interpretation of the ordinance.

# Chapter 9
# Appeals of Staff Decisions

The board of adjustment must hear and decide appeals from decisions of administrative officials concerning the zoning ordinance or the unified development ordinance. In addition, a local ordinance can assign the board of adjustment to hear appeals related to other development regulations.[1] These appeals require the board to interpret the ordinance and apply the ordinance to specific situations.

## Decisions That May Be Appealed

When zoning staff issues a "final and binding order, requirement, or determination,"[2] that decision may be appealed. These appealable decisions include a notice of violation, a formal interpretation of the ordinance, a zoning permit, and other final and binding determinations. Other staff actions are not formal decisions that can be appealed. A letter that merely states the basic zoning district of a property is not a binding decision—it is a recitation of the current rules. A verbal opinion (or even an email or letter) about how the ordinance *might* be interpreted is not a final binding determination subject to appeal. Inaction by staff is not a decision that can be appealed, but a party may seek a court order to require staff action that is not discretionary.

The local government official who made the decision that is being appealed must provide written notice of the decision to the property owner and the requesting party, if different from the owner. This written notice may be provided by personal delivery, email, or first-class mail.

---

1. G.S. 160A-388(b1).
2. G.S. 160A-388(a1).

## Parties and Standing

State law allows a party with standing to appeal a staff decision. As discussed in Chapter 3, that includes an individual with an ownership interest in the subject property, the applicant for a permit/recipient of a notice of violation (if different from the owner), the local government, and any person who will suffer special damages from the decision (as well as certain associations that have members who will suffer special damages).[3]

In appeals of staff decisions the role of staff is different from that in other types of quasi-judicial decisions. Whereas in a variance case or special use permit case a staff person may serve as a clerk and/or witness providing support and analysis for the board, in appeals of staff decisions the staff person acts as a party defending an interpretation of the ordinance. As discussed below, the staff person is required to compile and provide the record for the board and the appealing party and to appear as a witness for the hearing. This leads to heightened concerns of ex parte communications between the board and the staff person.

This dynamic of staff person as party also may complicate the role of the local government attorney who is called in to advise the board and the staff member who is appearing before the board. For this reason, some local governments assign separate attorneys, one for staff and one for the board, for appeals of staff decisions.

## Filing an Appeal

A person seeking to appeal a staff decision files with the local government clerk a notice of appeal stating the grounds for the appeal. An appeal of an enforcement action freezes that action except for certain limited situations outlined in state law.[4]

Parties have thirty days from notice of the decision to appeal. For a party receiving written notice from staff, the thirty-day period begins with receipt of the notice. For other parties, the thirty-day period begins with any notice—actual or constructive—of the decision. That notice could be a letter from the property owner, the beginning of construction on the

---

3. G.S. 160A-388(b1); G.S. 160A-393(d).
4. G.S. 160A-388(b1)(6).

site, or some other means of learning about the decision. If a party fails to appeal within thirty days, the board of adjustment cannot hear the appeal.

A property owner or developer who wants to start the clock for neighbor appeals can establish constructive notice for the neighbors by posting a sign on the property in question.[5] The sign must clearly state "Zoning Decision" or "Subdivision Decision" in letters at least six inches high and provide a way to contact an official about the decision. The sign must be posted for at least ten days, and the person posting the sign must provide verification of such posting to the official who made the decision. An ordinance may require such posted notice of decisions, but if not specified in the ordinance, it is an option for the property owner. Note that this sign to establish constructive notice is separate from the routine notice required in advance of any quasi-judicial hearing, including an appeal of a staff decision.

Instead of taking an appeal to the board of adjustment, the parties to an appeal may agree to mediation or other alternative dispute resolution. The ordinance may set standards and procedures to facilitate this process.

## Hearing and Record

The board of adjustment must hear and decide the appeal within a reasonable time, generally within two or three months of filing, though complicated cases can take longer. As with other quasi-judicial decisions, the board must provide notice (mailed and posted) and hold an evidentiary hearing to create the record upon which it will base its decision.

In advance of the hearing the official who made the decision being appealed must compile the record upon which he or she based the decision, including all applicable documents and exhibits. The official must provide that record to the board and a copy of the record to the individual appealing the decision and the property owner, if different.[6] The official who made the decision must attend the hearing as a witness.[7]

In some cases the party making the appeal, or the party's attorney, may submit in advance a written analysis (essentially a legal brief) for board

---

5. G.S. 160A-388(b1)(4).
6. G.S. 160A-388(b1)(5).
7. G.S. 160A-388(b1)(8).

consideration. If so, copies should be provided to the board and the parties just as the rest of the record is provided.

The extent to which new evidence is needed or appropriate depends on the case. In some cases, the facts are undisputed; the record as compiled by staff is sufficient. In these instances, the board does not need to take new evidence to decide contested facts, but, rather, it needs to hear legal arguments from the parties to decide a question of law. In an interpretation case, for example, the parties may agree to the basic facts (proposed building, applicable section of the ordinance, etc.) but disagree on the legal question of how to interpret the ordinance correctly (for example, does the proposed building qualify as a single-family home?).

In other cases, the board may need to supplement the record with additional facts in order to make the decision. In an appeal of a notice of violation, for example, the parties may dispute whether and when a certain land use occurred on the property. The property owner may have documents or testimony that challenges the record provided by staff. The evidentiary hearing may elicit additional evidence for the record, and the board must resolve contested facts in its decision.

At the hearing the appealing party may raise issues beyond what was stated in the notice of appeal, but if a party would be unduly prejudiced by the lack of notice of those issues, the board must continue the hearing.[8]

## The Decision

"The board of adjustment may reverse or affirm, wholly or partly, or may modify the decision appealed from and shall make any order, requirement, decision, or determination that ought to be made. The board shall have all the powers of the official who made the decision."[9] The decision must resolve contested facts, be based on competent, material, and substantial evidence in the record, and be provided to the parties as a written decision document.

---

8. G.S. 160A-388(b1)(8).
9. *Id.*

## Interpreting the Ordinance

Staff members and boards of adjustment must make interpretations about the meaning of the language in the ordinance and how it applies to particular situations. Ordinance language can be imprecise, and unanticipated situations arise. Below are some basic guidelines for interpreting the ordinance.

### Start with the Ordinance Text

When interpreting a local ordinance, the board must determine the intent of the governing board. The best way to determine that intent is from the text itself.[10] Where an "ordinance is clear and unambiguous, its plain meaning will be enforced."[11]

### Definitions

Many terms are defined in the ordinance, either in a general list of definitions or within specific sections, and the board must give meaning to and carry out those definitions when interpreting the ordinance. If a term is not defined in the ordinance, a dictionary should be consulted to derive the term's plain and ordinary meaning.[12] In one case, for example, the North Carolina Court of Appeals had to decide whether or not a property owner's activities—including weighing, grading, and storing cut timber—constituted "forestry" under the zoning ordinance. The term was not defined in the ordinance, so the court considered and quoted the definition of "forestry" from two dictionaries.[13]

### Ordinance Guidance

The ordinance itself may have rules of interpretation to guide whether and how the administrator should interpret and accommodate uses, how to resolve conflicts, and other topics of interpretation. As an example, when a town sought to enforce a special use permit provision over a general district

---

10. Bryan v. Wilson, 259 N.C. 107, 130 S.E.2d 68 (1963).

11. Pritchard v. Elizabeth City, 81 N.C. App. 543, 549, 344 S.E.2d 821, 824 (1986) (internal citation omitted).

12. Rice Assocs. v. Town of Weaverville Bd. of Adjustment, 108 N.C. App. 346, 423 S.E.2d 519 (1992).

13. Ayers v. Bd. of Adjustment for Town of Robersonville through Roberson, 113 N.C. App. 528, 532, 439 S.E.2d 199, 201–02 (1994).

provision, the court stressed the ordinance rule of construction that when there is conflict among ordinance provisions "the more restrictive provision shall apply."[14]

## Purpose and Intent Language

Purpose and intent language may be included for particular districts (like the industrial district) or for a particular provision (like provisions for sign regulations). This purpose language outlines the goals of the ordinance and may guide how the ordinance should be interpreted and enforced. In one case, the court considered whether a private military training facility was permitted in the local agricultural zoning district. The ordinance itself was not clear, so the court looked to the purpose language, among other things. The purpose language stated:

> A1 Agricultural District. This district is designed to promote and protect agricultural lands, including woodlands, within the County. *The general intent* of the district is to permit all agricultural uses to exist *free from most private urban development except for* large lot, single-family development. Some public and/or semi-public uses as well as *a limited list of convenient commercial uses are permitted to ensure essential services for the residents.*[15]

Based on the purpose language, as well as other interpretive guidance, the court determined that the training facility was not permitted.

## General Rules of Interpretation

Beyond the definitions and guidance of the ordinance itself, there are general rules of statutory interpretation that apply to ordinance interpretation. Following are descriptions of some of the most frequently used rules.

**Specific provisions control over general provisions.** In other words, greater weight is given to specific language than to general language in the ordinance.[16] So, for example, when an ordinance lists a specific use in the permitted use table, that controls over general language about the intent of the zoning district.

---

14. Westminster Homes, Inc. v. Town of Cary Zoning Bd. of Adjustment, 354 N.C. 298, 554 S.E.2d 634 (2001).

15. Fort v. Cty. of Cumberland, 218 N.C. App. 401, 406, 721 S.E.2d 350, 354 (2012) (emphasis added by the court).

16. *Westminster Homes*, 354 N.C. at 298, 554 S.E.2d at 634.

**Birds of a feather flock together.** An ambiguous term can be interpreted based on its association with other terms in the ordinance. When a list of specific terms is followed by a general term, the general term is considered to be of the same class or kind as of those it follows.[17] For example, if an ordinance lists "dogs, cats, fish and other pets," it is presumed that "other pets" would include common household domesticated animals, such as small birds, and not tigers or bears.

**Listing one thing is to the exclusion of others.** When an ordinance expressly includes certain terms, the suggestion is that it excludes others. If the ordinance allows household pets, the implication is that it does not allow livestock. This is particularly true if omitted items are specifically used in some other part of the ordinance.

**Give meaning and avoid absurdity.** Interpretations should not render any ordinance language irrelevant or superfluous.[18] Also, interpretations should not lead to absurd or bizarre results.[19] It would be bizarre, for example, if the ordinance was interpreted to prohibit all residential uses within the residential zoning district.

**Favor free use of land.** Finally, after all of the tools of interpretation are exhausted, ambiguity is resolved in favor of the property owner and the free use of land.[20]

17. Bryan v. Wilson, 259 N.C. 107, 130 S.E.2d 68 (1963).

18. Astoria Fed. Savings & Loan Ass'n v. Solimino, 501 U.S. 104 (1991).

19. State v. Jones, 359 N.C. 832, 616 S.E.2d 496 (2005).

20. Land v. Vill. of Wesley Chapel, 206 N.C. App. 123, 697 S.E.2d 458 (2010).

# Chapter 10
# Judicial Review

If an affected party believes the board making a quasi-judicial decision made a legal error, the decision can be appealed to court. The decision may not be appealed to the city council or board of county commissioners. The board that made the decision cannot be asked to reconsider its final decision absent a substantial change in the application, ordinance, or circumstances on the site. A final quasi-judicial decision can be challenged only by appealing to superior court (with the exception of an appeal of a decision on a certificate of appropriateness, which is initially reviewed by the board of adjustment).

## Petition for Judicial Review

Judicial review of quasi-judicial decisions is initiated by filing a petition for review with the clerk of superior court in the county where the land subject to the decision is located.

The petition for review is required to name as the respondent the local government whose board made the decision being appealed.[1] The board that actually made the decision is not the respondent; the local government is. The official name of one such case would be *Smith v. Town of Mayberry* rather than *Smith v. Board of Adjustment of the Town of Mayberry*. An exception to this rule can be made if the unit of government is itself bringing the challenge. So, for example, if the board of adjustment overrules a staff interpretation and the town council decides to challenge that decision in court, the name of the action would be *Town of Mayberry v. Board of Adjustment of the Town of Mayberry*. Very important to note is that if neighbors with standing challenge a quasi-judicial decision, the permit applicant also must be named as a respondent. If the petition does not name the applicant in this situation, the court has no jurisdiction to hear the appeal and must

---

1. G.S. 160A-393(e).

dismiss the case. A property owner or tenant who was not the applicant also may be named as a respondent, but that is not required.

The petition for review must contain the basic facts that establish the standing of the challenger to bring the suit, the grounds for the legal error alleged to have been made by the decision-making board, the facts that support any allegation of a conflict of interest, and the relief the person wants from the court, such as ordering that the decision be reversed.[2] The petition also is to include an order (known as a writ of certiorari). This order, which is then issued by the clerk of superior court, directs the city or county to prepare and submit to the court the record of the decision for the court's review. An example of a writ of certiorari issued for a case appealing a board of adjustment's decision on zoning ordinance interpretation is presented in Appendix D.

## Time to Bring a Challenge

The time for filing an appeal of a final quasi-judicial decision is thirty days. This is in contrast to the longer times allowed to file judicial challenges to legislative zoning decisions. In those instances a person with standing has two months to challenge a rezoning and a year to challenge the validity of an ordinance (measured from the time that standing is secured).

A key question is when the thirty-day period to challenge a quasi-judicial decision begins to run. It does not start on the date the vote is taken. Rather, the effective date of the decision and the date of its delivery are the critical dates. A judicial appeal must be filed with the clerk of court within the later of

1. thirty days from the effective date of the decision (when the signed decision is filed) or
2. thirty days from the delivery of the decision to those entitled to get a written copy. If the decision is sent by first-class mail, three days is added to the time it was deposited in the mail.

---

2. G.S. 160A-393(c).

## Standing

Only a person with legal standing is entitled to initiate judicial review of a quasi-judicial decision. State law defines whom this includes.[3] Those with standing are as follows:

1. the applicant or owner of the property involved (including lessees and persons with an option to purchase the property),
2. anyone else who would suffer special damages as a result of the decision,
3. a group or association if at least one of the members of the group would have standing and the group was not created in response to the development that is the subject of the appeal, and
4. the local government whose board made the decision being challenged.

When a challenge is made by someone else, any entity with standing can intervene in the case. For example, if a property owner challenges the denial of a special use permit, a neighbor with standing can intervene and participate in the case.

A critical question for standing is, what constitutes "special damages"? Being a resident or taxpayer in the jurisdiction is not sufficient. As discussed in Chapter 4 regarding standing to participate in the matter being considered by a decision-making board, a person seeking to participate in the judicial proceeding must show that he or she will likely be harmed by the decision in a way that is different from the impact on the general public or community at large. Key factors considered in whether there is a credible allegation of special damages include proximity to the property affected, impacts on property values, and such secondary impacts as harms caused by traffic, noise, stormwater runoff, and the like.[4]

---

3. G.S. 160A-393(d).
4. Mangum v. Raleigh Bd. of Adjustment, 362 N.C. 640, 669 S.E.2d 279 (2008).

## Standard for Review

When the superior court reviews a quasi-judicial decision, it is acting as an appeals court. There is no new evidentiary hearing. No additional evidence is taken by the court other than the narrow exception regarding legal issues noted below. Rather, the court looks to see if the hearing record supports the board's findings and conclusions. Legal issues, such as interpretation of the law, adherence to proper procedures, or impartiality of the decision-makers, also can be raised in judicial review.

State law specifies the content of the record to be assembled in appeals of quasi-judicial decisions.[5] The record is to include all documents and exhibits submitted to the decision-making board as well as the minutes of all meetings at which the matter was heard. If an audiotape or videotape of the meeting is available, any party may request that it be included in the record. Any party also may include a verbatim transcript of the meeting (the cost of preparing the transcript being the responsibility of the party choosing to include it). The record is prepared by the local government and is filed with the court conducting the review.[6] It must be bound and paginated. The record is then served on all petitioners by the local government within three days of filing it with the court.

The trial court is authorized to take new evidence in very limited circumstances. While the board may have ruled on objections regarding standing or alleged impermissible conflicts of interest, the court may, in its discretion, allow the record to be supplemented with affidavits or testimony regarding these issues. The court also may allow additional evidence regarding legal issues of constitutionality or statutory authority for the decision, since these legal questions are beyond the scope of issues that could have been addressed by the original decision-making board.[7]

When the court reviews the quasi-judicial decision that was made, it looks at the following issues:[8]

1. Whether it violated the constitutional rights of the parties. For example, were the requirements for a fair and impartial hearing observed?

---

5. G.S. 160A-393(i).

6. G.S. 160A-393(f).

7. G.S. 160A-393(j).

8. G.S. 160A-393(k); Coastal Ready-Mix Concrete Co. v. Bd. of Comm'rs, 299 N.C. 620, 265 S.E.2d 379 (1980).

2. Whether it was within the statutory authority of the local government.
3. Whether it followed the procedures set by state statutes and the ordinance involved.
4. Whether an error of law was made.
5. Whether there was substantial, competent, and material evidence in the hearing record to support the findings and conclusions made.
6. Whether the action taken was arbitrary and capricious.

On any legal issues to be resolved, such as constitutionality, scope of statutory authority, or interpretation of the statutes and ordinance, the court takes a fresh look at the issues and makes its own judgment. On a legal issue regarding interpretation of the ordinance, the court may consider the decision-making board's interpretation, but it is not bound by that, and the court may freely substitute its judgment on the correct interpretation. For example, a zoning ordinance may require the city council to find a proposed special use to be in harmony with the surrounding area without providing a specific definition of what the "surrounding area" is. To make its decision, the council must interpret what the geographic area is for its determination on the in harmony and compatible with requirement. On appeal, the court would consider how the council defined the "area," but the court is free to make its own interpretation of that ordinance term.

On the other hand, factual findings made by the decision-making board are binding on the court if they are supported by sufficient evidence in the record. Here the question for the court is not whether the board correctly decided contested facts, but whether there was substantial evidence in the record to support the findings that were made. For example, in considering a variance petition the board of adjustment may make factual findings as to the cost of complying with the applicable regulation—such as it would add $15,000 in construction costs if compliance is required. That finding on the costs would then be binding on the reviewing court if it is supported by testimony and records submitted at the board's hearing. On the other hand, whether an additional cost of $15,000 would be a "substantial hardship" in that particular case would be a question of law on which the court can make its own independent judgment.

## Action by the Court

Once its review is complete, the court has multiple options. It can affirm the decision that was made, reverse it, or remand the case to the board for further action.

If the court finds that a procedural error was made, it can send the case back for that error to be corrected. If it finds that the decision document failed to make adequate findings of fact but that the hearing record includes sufficient evidence to do so, it can send the case back to the board with a direction to make those findings solely on the evidence already in the record (without conducting an additional hearing).

If the hearing record supports it, the court can overrule a board's decision to deny a request and order that the request be approved. The court can also overrule a board's decision to approve a request and order that the approval be revoked if there was insufficient evidence in the record to support granting approval. Likewise, individual conditions that were imposed also can be modified or stricken by the court.

Appeals of the superior court's decision are made to the state court of appeals and proceed in the same manner as any civil appeal.

# Appendix A: Sample Application Forms

Application No._____

## CITY OF WILMINGTON
## STATE OF NORTH CAROLINA

### APPLICATION FOR A VARIANCE

**PURPOSE OF VARIANCE** – A Variance is the official allowance of a variation from the dimensional requirements of the City Land Development Code or other development regulations. An applicant for a variance must demonstrate valid reasons which create a need for a Variance. These reasons cannot be strictly economic in nature but must generally involve some physical problem with the subject property which will not allow it to be developed in a reasonable manner if City development regulations are followed literally, such as a lot which is substandard in area or width.

> **BOARD OF ADJUSTMENT** - The Board of Adjustment, or BOA, is the official City Board that considers requests for variances. The BOA receives sworn testimony at its meetings and issues decisions on variance requests based on this testimony. It is the responsibility of each applicant for a Variance to attend the BOA meeting and present sworn testimony in support of the request.

> **REASON FOR VARIANCE REQUEST** – Explain in your own words why you are requesting a Variance. Be sure to clearly indicate the problem(s) you will experience in complying with the City development regulations. (Attach additional sheets if needed.)

_____

_____

_____

The BOARD OF ADJUSTMENT is required to make the following four (4) findings before granting a Variance. Write a thorough response to each of these items.

1. Unnecessary hardship would result from the strict application of the ordinance. It shall not be necessary to demonstrate that, in the absence of the variance, no reasonable use can be made of the property;

2. The hardship results from conditions that are peculiar to the property, such as location, size, or topography. Hardships resulting from conditions that are common to the neighborhood or the general public may not be the basis for granting a variance;

3. The hardship did not result from actions taken by the applicant or the property owner. The act of purchasing property with knowledge that circumstances exist that may justify the granting of a variance shall not be regarded as a self-created hardship;

4. The requested variance is consistent with the spirit, purpose, and intent of the ordinance, such that public safety is secured, and substantial justice is achieved.

Application No._____

ATTACH PLOT PLAN DESCRIBING VARIANCE REQUEST

**PROPERTY LOCATION INFORMATION**

Street address of subject property _____

Tax Parcel Number of subject property _____

ATTACH TAX PARCEL & OWNERSHIP INFORMATION FOR ADJACENT
PROPERTIES (Include stamped, self-addressed envelopes)

APPLICANT INFORMATION                    OWNER INFORMATION
Name/Address/Telephone                    Name/Address/Telephone

_____          _____

_____          _____

_____          _____

ATTACH AGENT FORM IF THE APPLICANT IS NOT OWNER

DATE_____          APPLICANT'S SIGNATURE_____

## INFORMATION TO APPLICANTS APPEARING BEFORE
## THE CITY OF WILMINGTON BOARD OF ADJUSTMENT FOR A VARIANCE

The Board of Adjustment regularly meets on the third Thursday of each month at 1:00 p.m. in the First Floor Conference Room at City Hall, 102 North 3rd Street, Wilmington, NC.

An application to the Board of Adjustment for a variance must be submitted to the City of Wilmington Zoning Division, located at 305 Chestnut Street, 3rd Floor, **thirty (30) working days** prior to the meeting at which the application is to be considered. **Should the applicant or his agent fail to appear for a duly scheduled hearing before the Board of Adjustment without first requesting a continuance, such application for a variance may be dismissed by the Board.**

An application must be accompanied by the following items - otherwise, it will not be accepted.

1) A list of:
   (a) names of all adjacent property owners and their mailing addresses;
   (b) addresses of all adjacent properties; and
   (c) tax parcel numbers of all adjacent properties.

   Adjacent properties are all properties abutting the site and properties immediately across the street from it. An example is attached.

2) Stamped, letter size envelopes (4" x 9-1/2") addressed to all adjacent property owners and bearing the return address of the City of Wilmington Zoning Division, P.O. Box 1810, Wilmington, NC, 28402-1810.

3) A check made payable to the City of Wilmington in the amount of $500.00 for a variance request and for all other appeals.

4) Completed application form (including plot plan showing the nature of the variance request) and completed agent form, if needed. NOTE: The plot plan shall be drawn to scale and its size shall not exceed 11" x 17". Two (2) larger site plans, 24" x 36", must also be submitted for presentation purposes.

5) A New Hanover County tax map delineating the property in question.

Please contact the Zoning Division at 254-0900 if you have any questions.

FM BOA Inf to Appl 6/02 AC
/kht

## WILMINGTON
NORTH CAROLINA

## APPLICATION ACCEPTANCE POLICY

BOARD OF ADJUSTMENT – REQUEST FOR VARIANCE

City of Wilmington
Planning, Development and Transportation
Zoning Division

PO Box 1810 | 305 Chestnut St.
Wilmington, NC 28402
Telephone 910.254.0900 | Fax 910.341.3264

The City of Wilmington understands that clear expectations make the application and review processes easier for both applicants and staff. The policies outlined below will enable staff to move the process along in a way that ensures that each application receives the attention it deserves. Staff desires to complete review of projects in an accurate and timely manner. Due to the volume of applications and public hearing schedules, working with incomplete materials detracts from the timely review of applications.

1. Applications are to be reviewed for completeness by staff prior to being officially accepted by the City for review. Applications that are dropped off or mailed in cannot be accepted without prior approval from the Zoning Administrator.

2. Checklists for each type of request are provided with each application package. If the application does not contain all required items on the checklist, it will be considered incomplete and shall not be accepted.

3. Upon determination by staff that an application for a variance is complete, it will be officially accepted by the Zoning Division. Staff will complete an acceptance form and both staff and the applicant must sign the form. The application is not considered officially accepted until this form is signed by both the planner and the applicant. A copy of the signed form will be given to the applicant and a copy will be placed in the project file at the time of acceptance. Staff will not hold materials for incomplete applications.

4. Application fees must be paid at the time an application is submitted for acceptance.

5. In order to allow time to process fees, applications will not be accepted after 4:00 PM each day. On the deadline day for submittals for Board of Adjustment hearings, applications will not be accepted after 1:00 PM.

6. For your convenience, applicants may schedule an appointment with staff or may "walk-in" without an appointment. Please allow sufficient time to review the application package with staff.

The Planning Division staff looks forward to working with you during the application process. If you have questions or need further assistance, please call 254-0900.

❑

R:\Application Intake forms\Policies\Data\BOA Policy Variances.doc

## VARIANCE OR APPEAL APPLICATION

**TOWN OF CHAPEL HILL**
**Planning Department**
405 Martin Luther King Jr. Blvd
phone (919) 968-2728          fax (919) 969-2014
www.townofchapelhill.org

Parcel Identifier Number (PIN): _____    Date: _____

### Section A: Project Information

Project Name: _____

Property Address: _____    Zip Code: _____

Existing Zoning District: _____

Project Description: _____
_____
_____

### Section B: Applicant, Owner and/or Contract Purchaser Information

**Applicant Information** (to whom correspondence will be mailed)

Name: _____

Address: _____

City: _____    State: _____    Zip Code: _____

Phone: _____    Email: _____

The undersigned applicant hereby certifies that, to the best of his knowledge and belief, all information supplied with this application is true and accurate.

Signature: _____    Date: _____

**Owner/Contract Purchaser Information:**

☐ Owner          ☐ Contract Purchaser

Name: _____

Address: _____

City: _____    State: _____    Zip Code: _____

Phone: _____    Email: _____

The undersigned applicant hereby certifies that, to the best of his knowledge and belief, all information supplied with this application is true and accurate.

Signature: _____    Date: _____

Revised 12.08.10                    Parcel Identifier Number (PIN):_____

**VARIANCE OR APPEAL APPLICATION**
**SUBMITTAL REQUIREMENTS**
TOWN OF CHAPEL HILL
Planning Department

Variances and Appeals may be granted by the Board of Adjustment for dimensional regulations, water and sewer regulations, steep slope regulations, house size limitations, Resource Conservation District regulations, Jordan Buffer regulations, and Watershed Protection District regulations. The following must accompany your application. Failure to do so will result in your application being considered incomplete. For assistance with this application, please contact the Chapel Hill Planning Department (Planning) at (919)968-2728 or at planning@townofchapelhill.org. For detailed information, please refer to the Description of Detailed Information handout.

|  | **Application fee** (refer to fee schedule) | Amount Paid $ |
|---|---|---|
|  | **Digital Files** - provide digital files of all plans and documents | |
|  | **Mailing list of owners of property within 1,000 feet perimeter of subject property** (see GIS notification tool) | |
|  | **Mailing fee for above mailing list** | Amount Paid $ |
|  | **Written Narrative describing the proposal** | |
|  | **Statement of Justification** – see below for additional information | |
|  | **Recorded Plat or Deed of Property** | |
|  | **Stream Determination** - necessary for all submittals | |
|  | **Jurisdictional Wetland Determination** – if applicable | |
|  | **Reduced Site Plan Set (reduced to 8.5"x11")** | |

## Type of Variance or Appeal (Choose one of the following):

☐ **Dimensional Variance**      ☐ **Water and Sewer Variance**      ☐ **Steep Slope Variance**

Statement of Justification: Respond to parts 1-7 of Subsection 4.12.2(a) of the Land Use Management Ordinance

☐ **House Size Variance**

Statement of Justification: Respond to parts 1-7 of Subsection 4.12.2(b) of the Land Use Management Ordinance

☐ **Resource Conservation District Variance**

Statement of Justification: Respond to parts A-I of Subsection 3.6.3(j)(4) of the Land Use Management Ordinance

☐ **Jordan Watershed Riparian Buffer Variance**

Statement of Justification: Respond to parts A-C of Subsection 5.18.8(d)(1) of the Land Use Management Ordinance

☐ **Watershed Protection District Variance**

Statement of Justification: Respond to parts 1-4 of Subsection 3.6.4(h)(2) of the Land Use Management Ordinance

☐ **Appeal**

Standing: Explain to the Board how the applicant is an aggrieved party (NC General Statute Sec. 160A-388(b1)(1)
Statement of Justification: Provide justification for decision that is being appealed

**VARIANCE OR APPEAL APPLICATION**
**SUBMITTAL REQUIREMENTS**
TOWN OF CHAPEL HILL
Planning Department

## Plan Sets (20 copies to be submitted no larger than 24"x36")

Plans should be legible and clearly drawn.  All plan sets sheets should include the following:
- Project Name
- Legend
- Labels
- North Arrow (North oriented toward top of page)
- Property Boundaries with bearing and distances
- Scale (Engineering), denoted graphically and numerically
- Setbacks
- Streams, RCD Boundary, Jordan Riparian Buffer Boundary, Floodplain, and Wetlands Boundary, where applicable

**Area Map**

   a)      Overlay Districts
   b)      1,000 foot notification boundary

**Detailed Site Plan**

Revised 12.08.10              Parcel Identifier Number (PIN):_____

# Appendix B: Sample Mailed Notice

DURHAM

1869
CITY OF MEDICINE

CITY OF DURHAM | DURHAM COUNTY
NORTH CAROLINA

DCO
DURHAM
COUNTY

Dear Property Owner or Registered Neighborhood Organization Representative:

The Durham Board of Adjustment will hold a public hearing on _____[date] at 8:30 a.m in the Committee Room, 101 City Hall Plaza, 2nd floor, on the following request:

**Case** _____: A variance _____. The subject site is located at _____, is zoned _____, and is in the _____. PIN: _____.

This is a quasi-judicial hearing, very similar to a court hearing. All testimony must be sworn and in person before the Board. Comments called in and letters or written statements [such as petitions] cannot be entered into the record. Having first-hand testimony allows for cross-examination of all witnesses by the Board and others in attendance. Testimony offered on the case should be from direct personal or professional knowledge, and focused on the ordinance-specified considerations of the Board. If several people have testimony to offer, it is suggested they coordinate their efforts to avoid repetition. Note: This is not a zone change request. Changes to the proposed action may be made by the Board following the public hearing.

The applications and maps may be reviewed at the City-County Planning Department, 101 City Hall Plaza, Ground Floor, between 8:00 a.m. and 4:30 p.m. The staff reports may be viewed at http://durhamnc.gov/AgendaCenter/Board-of-Adjustment-BOA-10 Tuesday, one week prior to the meeting or may be picked up in the City-County Planning Department at 101 City Hall Plaza, Ground Floor.

An appeal to the Board of Adjustment action can be filed pursuant to procedures noted in the North Carolina General Statutes, Chapter 160A, Article 19, Part 3, Section 160A-388 or Chapter 153A, Article 18, part 3, Section 153A-345.

All decisions of the Board of Adjustment are subject to appeal to Superior Court within 30 days after the aggrieved party receives the Board's written decision. Anyone wishing to receive a copy of the written decision on this case must file a written request with the Planning staff at or before the hearing. Forms for such a request will be available at the hearing or from the Planning staff prior to the hearing.

If you have questions, please contact me between 8:30 a.m. and 4:30 p.m. at [phone number] or [email address], or visit our website at http://durhamnc.gov/338/City-County-Planning. Please reference the case number when calling.

Sincerely,

_____, Planner

**Notice under the Americans with Disabilities Act -** A person with a disability may receive an auxiliary aid or service to effectively participate in city government activities by contacting the ADA Coordinator, voice 919.560.4197 or ADA@DurhamNC.gov, as soon as possible but no later than 48 hours before the event or deadline date.

# Appendix C: Sample Subpoena for Quasi-Judicial Proceedings

NORTH CAROLINA )
                  )        WINSTON-SALEM ZONING BOARD OF ADJUSTMENT
FORSYTH COUNTY)

                  )        APPEAL OF ASSESSMENT OF CIVIL PENALTY
    **SUBPOENA**   )
                  )              CASE NUMBER #_____

TO:      _____
         _____
         _____

    Upon the request and a majority vote of the Winston-Salem Zoning Board of Adjustment, and pursuant to N.C. Gen. Stat. § 160A-388(g), you are hereby ordered to appear at the regularly scheduled Zoning Board of Adjustment public hearing at _____[time and date], to testify before the Board in the matter of the appeal filed by _____ [appealing party].

    The hearing will be conducted in the Public Meeting Room of the Bryce A. Stuart Municipal Building, Fifth Floor, 100 E. First Street, Winston-Salem, NC 27101.

    This the ____ day of _____, 2016.


                          _____
                          _____, Chairman
                          City of Winston-Salem Zoning Board of Adjustment

# Appendix D: Sample from a Writ of Certiorari

NORTH CAROLINA

CHATHAM COUNTY

IN THE GENERAL COURT OF JUSTICE
SUPERIOR COURT DIVISION
16 CVS 457

CHATHAM COUNTY, a North Carolina
County,

Petitioner,

v.

CHATHAM COUNTY BOARD OF
ADJUSTMENT, APEX NURSERIES,
INC., JEAN R. COPELAND, KAREN
DENISE COPELAND AND WILLIAM
RAGAN COPELAND,

Respondents.

**WRIT OF CERTIORARI**

This cause coming to be heard *ex parte* before the undersigned Clerk or Assistant Clerk
of Superior Court for Chatham County, North Carolina, upon a Petition for Writ of Certiorari,
and this Court, finding the Writ should be allowed pursuant to N.C. Gen. Stat. § 153A-349
and § 160A-393(f);

IT IS HEREBY ORDERED, ADJUDGED AND DECREED:

1.     The Respondent Chatham County Board of Adjustment shall prepare and certify
to this Court the complete record of all proceedings relating in any way to the Chatham County
Board of Adjustment's written decision filed on June 1, 2016 dismissing three Notices of
Violation dated October 14, 2015 and reversing a related zoning interpretation issued by the
Zoning Administrator dated March 7, 2016.

2.     That the Respondent Chatham County Board of Adjustment shall cause a true

Carolina, within sixty (60) days from and after receipt of a copy of this Writ of Certiorari and shall simultaneously serve a copy thereof on counsel for the Petitioner and other Respondents;

3. That the Petitioner shall serve the Petition for Writ of Certiorari and the Writ of Certiorari upon Respondents in the manner provided for service of a complaint under Rule 4(j) of the North Carolina Rules of Civil Procedure, except that no summons shall be issued.

This the _30_ day of _June_, 2016.

_Brenda Shaw_
Clerk/Assistant Clerk of Superior Court
Chatham County

Page **2** of **2**

# Appendix E: Chair's Script for Meetings and Evidentiary Hearings

This sample script offers basic guidance and language for how a board chairperson may guide a quasi-judicial evidentiary hearing. This sample is necessarily generic. Local governments must tailor this language to their local rules, policies, and standards.

### I. Start the Meeting

"The meeting will now come to order. Welcome to this meeting of the _____ [insert board name] on _____ [date]. My name is _____ [insert chair name], and I am chair of the board. Would the board members please go around and state their name for the record?"

*PAUSE*

"_____ [insert staff name] is serving as staff to the board today. Also, attorney _____ will be advising the board on legal and procedural questions.

"We will follow the order printed on the agenda. You can find a copy of the agenda and a guide to meeting procedures at _____ [insert location of materials]. Also, if you wish to speak as a witness today, you can find the sign-up sheet there."

### II. Adopt Minutes

"We will consider the minutes from the last meeting of the board. Are there any questions or corrections?"

*PAUSE*

"Is there a motion to approve the minutes of the last meeting?"

*MOTION, SECOND, DISCUSSION, AND VOTE*

## III. General Introduction to Quasi-Judicial Decisions

"We now open the evidentiary hearing for _____ [insert name of case and case number]. The applicant has requested _____ [insert special use permit, variance, etc.]. The property is located at _____ [insert address]."

[For variance hearing] "A four-fifths vote of the board is required to grant a variance."

[For all other hearings] "The decision will be made by a simple majority vote of the board."

"This hearing is a quasi-judicial evidentiary hearing. That means it is like a court hearing. State law sets specific procedures and rules concerning how this board must make its decision. These rules are different from other types of land use decisions like rezoning cases.

"The board's discretion is limited. The board must base its decision upon competent, relevant, and substantial evidence in the record. A quasi-judicial decision is not a popularity contest. It is a decision constrained by the standards in the ordinance and based on the facts presented. If you will be speaking as a witness, please focus on the facts and standards, not personal preference or opinion.

"Participation is limited. This meeting is open to the public. Everyone is welcome to watch. Parties with standing have rights to participate fully. Parties may present evidence, call witnesses, and make legal arguments. Parties are limited to the applicant, the local government, and individuals who can show they will suffer special damages. Other individuals may serve as witnesses when called by the board. General witness testimony is limited to facts, not opinions. For certain topics, this board needs to hear opinion testimony from expert witnesses. These topics include projections about impacts on property values and projections about impacts of increased traffic. Individuals providing expert opinion must be qualified as experts and provide the factual evidence upon which they base their expert opinion.

"Witnesses must swear or affirm their testimony. At this time, we will administer the oath for all individuals who intend to provide witness testimony.

"Do you solemnly swear or affirm that the evidence you shall give to the board in this action shall be the truth, the whole truth, and nothing but the truth [so help you God]?"

## IV. Disclosure

"The parties to this case are entitled to an impartial board. A board member may not participate in this hearing if she or he has a fixed opinion about the matter, a financial interest in the outcome of the matter, or a close relationship with an affected person. Does any board member have any partiality to disclose and recusal to offer?"

*PAUSE*

*IF THERE IS A RECUSAL*

"It is the policy of this board that a recused member shall step down from the dais and _____ [insert "have a seat with the general public"; "be excused from the room"; other policy]. The board member may return to the dais for the next matter.

*PROCEED TO EX PARTE COMMUNICATION*

"The parties to this case have rights for any ex parte communication to be disclosed. Ex parte communication is any communication about the case outside of the hearing. That may include site visits as well as conversations with parties, staff, or the general public. Does any board member have any site visits to disclose?"

*PAUSE*

"Does any board member have any conversations or other communications to disclose?"

*PAUSE*

"Based on the disclosures we've heard from the board concerning partiality and ex parte communications, does any member of the board or any party to this matter have an objection to a board member's participation in this hearing?"

*PAUSE*

*IF NOT, PROCEED WITH HEARING*

*IF A PARTY RAISES AN OBJECTION*

"_____ [insert party] has objected to _____'s [insert board member's name] participation in the hearing based on _____ [insert basis of objection]. When there is an objection to a board member participating in a quasi-judicial decision, the dispute is resolved by a majority vote of the remaining members of the board. I'll now ask the remaining members of the board for a motion as to whether _____ [insert board member's name] may participate in this hearing."

## V. Staff Presentation

"_____ [staff person] will introduce this hearing. Before you start please confirm that you were sworn at the start of the hearing. If not, I will administer the oath now."

*NOTE: Staff to summarize the request, state the applicable standards, recite notice provided, state what materials were provided to the board in advance, and summarize content of any staff analysis. In appeals of staff decisions, the staff person acts as a party to the case rather than in the typical role of staff to the board.*

## VI. Applicant Testimony and Argument

*NOTE: Additional language regarding standing, limiting wit-nesses, qualifying experts, and verifying documents is provided below under "Script for Particular Situations of Witnesses and Documentary Evidence."*

"The applicant, _____ [insert applicant name], will now present evidence and legal arguments in support of the request. As a reminder, any evidence and argument must focus upon the applicable standards.

"Before you begin, please state for the record your name, address, and relation to the case."

*PAUSE*

"Please confirm that you were sworn at the start of the hearing. If not, I will administer the oath now."

*TESTIMONY AND LEGAL ARGUMENT*

"Does the board have questions for the witness?"

*PAUSE*

"Does any party have additional questions for the witness?"

*PAUSE*

"_____ [insert applicant name], do you wish to call any other witnesses to speak on behalf of your case?"

*APPLICANT MAY CALL ADDITIONAL WITNESSES*

"Before you begin, please state for the record your name, address and relation to the case."

*PAUSE*

"Please confirm that you were sworn at the start of the hearing. If not, I will administer the oath now."

*TESTIMONY*

"Does the board have questions for the witness?"

*PAUSE*

"Does any party have additional questions for this witness?"

*PAUSE*

## VII. Other Parties with Standing Testimony and Argument (if any)

*STANDING DETERMINATION, IF NEEDED (scripted below, under Particular Situations).*

"_____ [insert name of other party with standing] will now present evidence and legal arguments for or against the request. As a reminder, any evidence and argument must focus upon the applicable standards.

"Before you begin, please state for the record your name, address, and relation to the case."

*PAUSE*

"Please confirm that you were sworn at the start of the hearing. If not, I will administer the oath now."

*TESTIMONY AND LEGAL ARGUMENT*

"Does the board have questions for the witness?"

*PAUSE*

"Does any party have additional questions for the witness?"

*PAUSE*

"_____ [insert party name], do you wish to call any other witnesses to speak on behalf of your case?"

*PARTY MAY CALL ADDITIONAL WITNESSES*

"Before you begin, please state for the record your name, address, and relation to the case."

*PAUSE*

"Please confirm that you were sworn at the start of the hearing. If not, I will administer the oath now."

*TESTIMONY*

"Does the board have questions for the witness?"

*PAUSE*

"Does any party have additional questions for this witness?"

*PAUSE*

## VIII. Other Witness Testimony (if any)

"We will hear from other individuals wishing to provide factual testimony concerning the request.

"As a reminder, witnesses should provide factual testimony as to how this project does or does not meet the standards. The board must base its decision upon evidence in the record. Not personal preference or opinion.

"Please be aware that the applicant and any other parties have certain rights to object to your testimony and cross-examine you as a witness. The board, though, will determine what evidence to consider and how much weight to assign it.

"I will call each witness individually."

*CALL WITNESS*

"Before you begin, please state for the record your name, address, and relation to the case."

*PAUSE*

"Please confirm that you were sworn at the start of the hearing. If not, I will administer the oath now."

*TESTIMONY*

"Does the board have questions for the witness?"

*PAUSE*

"Does any party wish to cross-examine the witness?"

*PAUSE*

## IX. Response

"Parties with standing have an opportunity to offer rebuttal or closing argument. As a reminder, please focus your response on legal arguments and new or clarifying evidence. Please avoid mere repetition of the evidence we already heard. We will begin with the applicant. Then, I will call any other parties with standing."

*CALL APPLICANT*

*CALL OTHER PARTIES*

## X. Motion to Continue the Hearing

"In limited circumstances this board may decide to continue a hearing to a later meeting. This may be at the request of a party or on the board's own motion. Does any party or a council member believe that a situation existed that warrants the continuance of this hearing? And is there a motion to continue?"

*PAUSE*

*MOTION, SECOND, DISCUSSION, AND VOTE*

*WITH VOTE TO CONTINUE THE HEARING*

"This hearing is continued to _____ [state time and place for the continued hearing]."

*NOTE: If the above happens and the issue is continued, then move to the next agenda item. If not, proceed with the following steps.*

## XI. Deliberation

"Does the board have any more questions for the parties or witnesses before we move into deliberation?

"Does any board member have personal knowledge of additional facts relevant to this case that should be entered into the record?"

*PAUSE*

"Hearing no additional questions or presentation of relevant facts, the board will now begin deliberation. The evidentiary hearing remains open so that the board may ask clarifying questions, if needed.

"As a reminder, this board is tasked with deciding if, based on the evidence presented, this proposal meets the applicable standards. This decision cannot be based on the personal preference of board members. Rather it is based on standards and evidence.

"Board members are encouraged to reference the applicable standards and specific evidence in their deliberation.

"For this particular case, the board is asked to decide: Does the record include competent, relevant, and substantial evidence that [insert standards for the request]?"

## XII. Motion and Vote

*NOTE: Board members may use draft motion. Board may vote on findings and decision separately or jointly.*

"Is there a motion to approve, approve with conditions, or deny the request?"

*MOTION, SECOND, DISCUSSION, AND VOTE*

## XIII. Decision and Closing

"Staff will draft and I (or an authorized designee) will sign a final written decision to reflect the vote and reasoning for this decision. That written decision will be provided to the applicant and other parties with a right to such notice. Parties have thirty days to appeal this decision.

"Thank you to everyone attending the hearing regarding _____ [insert case name]. We welcome you to stay for the other items on the agenda. If you are leaving, please do so quietly at this time."

## XIV. Script for Particular Situations of Witnesses and Documentary Evidence

### A. Standing Determination (if any)

"In order to act as a party in this case, an individual must have legal standing. The applicant, property owner, and local government have standing. Other individuals may have standing if they will suffer special damages. Evidence of standing may include proximity to the subject property, damage to property values, and secondary impacts from the requested development.

"If you wish to act as a party, please provide evidence to establish that you will suffer special damages from the requested development."

*SPEAKER OFFERS EVIDENCE*

"Does any party have additional evidence or questions for the speaker?"

*PAUSE*

"Is there a motion regarding whether _____ has standing in this matter?"

*MOTION, SECOND, DISCUSSION, AND VOTE*

### B. Limiting Witness Testimony

*FOR OPINION TESTIMONY*

"As a reminder, your testimony must be focused on factual evidence concerning the applicable standards. This board must base its decision on factual evidence in the record, not personal opinions."

*FOR REPETITIVE TESTIMONY*

"The board appreciates your testimony. Other witnesses have already introduced this information into the record. Unless you have different evidence, we will have to move on to the next witness."

C. Qualification for Expert Witness (if any)

"For certain technical matters this board needs opinion testimony from a qualified expert. Please state for the record your name, company, and address. Also, please state the topic(s) that you will discuss and provide your professional qualifications and experience that qualify you as an expert in this matter."

*PAUSE*

"With regard to the witness's status as an expert, do any parties with standing have any questions, any opposing evidence, or any objections?"

*NOTE: The board or chair (depending on the rules) decides whether a witness is an expert.*

D. Considering Documents

"Please confirm for the record, were these handouts provided earlier and are they already included in the record?"

*PAUSE*

[If new] "Staff will label and enter the evidence into the record. The board may choose to continue the item to next meeting so the handouts can be reviewed.

"The board needs confirmation that evidence is sufficiently trustworthy to be relied upon. To that end witnesses must authenticate documentary evidence submitted for the record."

*FOR A PHOTOGRAPH*

"Please testify for the record, when and where was the photograph taken?"

*PAUSE*

"Does the photograph fairly and accurately represent the subject depicted at the time the photograph was taken?"

*PAUSE*

*FOR A DOCUMENT*

"Please testify for the record, what is the source of this document, who is the author or creator, and what is the date of publication?"

*PAUSE*

"Is the document certified as authentic by signature or otherwise by the custodian of the record OR, do you have first-hand knowledge of the date of creation and author or creator of this document? Please testify for the record."

*PAUSE*

"If this is a copy, is this a true and accurate copy of the original as far as you know? Please testify for the record."

*PAUSE*

# Appendix F: Sample Rules of Procedure for Boards of Adjustment

Town of _____, North Carolina

Adopted: _____ [Date]

Amended: _____ [Dates]

I. GENERAL RULES.

The function of the Board of Adjustment (referred to as the "Board" in these Rules of Procedure) is to hear and determine certain quasi-judicial matters under the development regulations of the Town of _____.

The Board shall be governed by the terms of Chapter 160A, Article 19, Part 3 of the General Statutes of North Carolina and by the Unified Development Ordinance of the Town of _____ (referred to as the "UDO" in these Rules of Procedure).[1] The Board shall exercise such additional authority as may be given it under general law, special act and local ordinance. These rules of procedures are intended to supplement and explain procedural provisions and requirements set out in the applicable provisions of law and ordinance.

These rules of procedure are adopted by the Board under its authority as spelled out in Section _____ of the UDO.

All members of the Board shall thoroughly familiarize themselves with the statutes and ordinances specified above and these rules of procedure.

II. OFFICERS AND THEIR DUTIES.

A.    Chair. The Chair shall be a regular member elected by a majority vote of the full membership of the board (including extraterritorial and alternate members).[2] The Chair's term of office shall be one

---

1. This reference should be to the zoning ordinance, unified development ordinance, or other applicable local ordinance.

2. Alternatives are to have the officers appointed by the governing board or elected only by the regular members of the board.

year, or until a successor is elected, beginning on July 1. The Chair shall be eligible for reelection.[3] That Chair shall decide upon all points of order and procedure, subject to these rules. The Chair shall rule on all objections to the presentation of evidence. Rulings of the Chair may be appealed by a member of the Board to the full Board. The Chair shall appoint any committees found necessary to conduct the business of the Board.

B. Vice Chair. The Vice Chair shall be a regular member of the board elected by the Board in the same manner and for the same term as the Chair. The Vice-Chair shall serve as Acting Chair in the absence of the Chair and at such times the Vice-Chair shall have the same powers and duties as the Chair.

C. Interim Chair. In the event neither the Chair nor the Vice-Chair is available for a particular case or meeting, the Board shall elect one of its members to serve as Interim Chair for that case or meeting. At such times the Interim Chair shall have the same powers and duties as the Chair. Should the Chair or Vice-Chair arrive while an Interim Chair is presiding, the Interim Chair shall relinquish all duties with regard to presiding at the earliest point at which such transition may orderly proceed.

D. Secretary. The Secretary shall be the appointed Zoning Administrator for the Town of _____.[4] The Secretary, subject to the direction of the Chair and the Board, shall keep all records, shall conduct all correspondence of the Board, shall arrange for all public notices required to be given, shall notify members of pending meetings and their agenda, shall notify parties to cases before the Board of its decision on such cases, and shall generally supervise clerical work of the Board. The Secretary shall keep in a permanent volume the summary of minutes of every meeting of the Board. These shall show the record of all important facts pertaining

---

3. An alternative provision to unlimited terms for officers: *"No one shall serve as an officer for more than two consecutive full terms. Following a one-year absence, an individual is eligible to serve again as an officer."*

4. Alternatives are to appoint the planning director, city or county clerk, or some other staff person to be the secretary. In the absence of staff support, the rules would need to direct the board to elect one of its members as secretary as these essential functions must be performed.

to each meeting and hearing, every resolution acted upon by the Board and all votes of members of the Board upon any resolution or upon the final determination of any question, indicating the names of the members absent or failing to vote. The Secretary shall not be eligible to vote upon any matter.

The Secretary shall provide to every new member of the Board print or electronic copies of all relevant ordinances, these Rules of Procedure, and such other educational materials deemed appropriate. The Secretary shall arrange for an orientation for new members and shall coordinate provision of continuing education for Board members.

E.   Clerk. A clerk may be appointed by the Secretary. The clerk shall perform such tasks as may be assigned by the Chair or Secretary and shall assist the Secretary generally in the performance of the clerical work of the Board. The clerk shall not be eligible to vote upon any matter. If a clerk to the board is not designated, the Secretary shall perform the duties of the clerk.

III. MEMBERS.

A.   Regular Members. There shall be five[5] regular members of the Board, each to be appointed by the Town Council. The term of membership shall be three years. Terms begin on July 1. A member shall continue to serve until a replacement member is appointed and takes office. Members shall be eligible for reappointment.[6] To the extent feasible, the terms of members shall be staggered. Vacancies shall be filled by appointment by the Town Council, with the appointee serving the balance of the replaced member's term.

Regular members receiving notice of a meeting which they cannot attend or upon learning that they will be unable to participate in a particular case shall promptly give notice to the Secretary that they are unable to attend or to participate. The member shall, if feasible, provide that notice to the Secretary at least two working days prior to the date of the hearing.

---

5. G.S. 160A-388(a) requires that a board of adjustment have at least five members. A higher number of members can be set by local ordinance.

6. An alternate provision if term limits are desired: *"No regular member shall serve more than two complete consecutive terms."*

B.   Alternate Members.[7] There shall be two (2)[8] alternate members of the board, each appointed by the Town Council in the same manner as provided for regular members. Alternate members shall be encouraged to attend all meetings of the Board, but shall participate in hearing, deliberating, and deciding a case only when acting in the place of a regular member.[9] On receiving such notice that a regular member will not be participating, the Secretary shall, by the most expeditious means, notify an alternate member to attend. An alternate member shall be called upon by the Chair to participate in an individual case in the place of a member who has a conflict and is ineligible to participate in that case. Assignments shall be rotated between the alternate members except that the alternate appointed from the extraterritorial jurisdiction shall be called first when the regular member from the extraterritorial area is unavailable.

At any meeting or case upon which they are called upon to participate, alternate members shall have the same powers and duties as regular members. Alternate members who are present and participate in hearing an individual case shall continue to hear, deliberate and vote on that case at any subsequent meeting.

C.   Extraterritorial Members.[10] When the town has extraterritorial jurisdiction, it shall have extraterritorial regular and alternate members appointed as mandated by North Carolina General

---

7. An optional provision: *"Alternate members are allowed but not required by state statutes."* It is highly advisable to have alternate members to allow the board to function when members are absent or have a conflict in a particular case.

8. The number of alternate members desired may vary, depending on the size of the board and the frequency with which alternate members are needed in a particular jurisdiction.

9. As alternate members need to be fully familiar with the work of the board, many local governments encourage attendance at all meetings. This is also a useful provision as there may be an unexpected absence or an unanticipated conflict of interest for a regular member. An alternative provision if it is desired that alternate members only attend if needed: *"Alternate members of the Board shall be called upon to attend only those meetings and hearings at which one or more regular members are absent or unable to participate in the hearing of a case because of financial or other interest."*

10. This section should be included only for cities that have extraterritorial planning and development jurisdiction. It is not applicable to counties.

Statute 160A-362. Extraterritorial members shall have the right to participate in all matters and cases before the Board.[11]

IV. RULES OF CONDUCT FOR MEMBERS.

A. In accordance with the Unified Development Ordinance, members of the Board may be removed by the Town Council for cause, including violation of the rules stated below. The Chair shall report to the Town Council any violation of these rules of conduct.[12] Where feasible, the Town Council shall notify a member being considered for removal of the reasons for removal and give that member an opportunity to respond.

B. Faithful attendance at all meetings of the Board and conscientious performance of the duties required of members of the Board shall be considered a prerequisite for continuing membership on the Board. Any regular Board member who is absent for more than three consecutive regular meetings or more than half of the regular meetings in a calendar year shall lose his or her status as a Board member.[13] Absence due to sickness, death in the immediate family, or other emergencies of a similar nature shall be recognized as excused absences and shall not affect a member's status on the Board, except that in the event of a long illness or other such cause for prolonged absence the member shall be replaced. The clerk to the Board shall keep a record of attendance and shall provide reasonable notice to any member who is in immediate risk of failing to meet these attendance requirements.

C. Board members should disclose at the hearing any pertinent facts about a pending case of which they have personal knowledge prior

11. G.S. 160A-362 provides that the ordinance may allow extraterritorial jurisdiction (ETJ) members to participate in all matters. If the ordinance does not provide for this, this statute provides that ETJ members participate only on cases arising in the ETJ area.

12. Alternative provision if it is desired that the full board address violations of the rules of conduct: *The Board may by majority vote request that a member's position be vacated for cause and a replacement member appointed by the Town Council.*

13. Some rules set a higher threshold of minimum attendance, such as requiring attendance for at least 75 percent of the meetings held in a calendar year. Some rules also apply an attendance standard for alternate members if they are encouraged or required to attend meetings.

to the hearing. Other than this type of disclosure, a board member seated for a hearing should not testify at that hearing. A board member who is recused from a case should avoid testifying as a witness in that hearing if at all feasible.[14]

D.    Board members shall not participate in or vote on any quasi-judicial matter in a manner that would violate affected persons' constitutional rights to an impartial decision-maker. Impermissible conflicts include, but are not limited to, a member having a fixed opinion prior to hearing the matter that is not susceptible to change; undisclosed ex parte communications; a close, familial, business, or other associational relationship with an affected person; or a financial interest in the outcome of the matter.[15] Board members shall endeavor to avoid the appearance of impropriety. A member with a potential bias or conflict of interest may consult with the Chair, the Secretary, or the Town Attorney regarding that potential conflict prior to the hearing. A Board member with a bias or conflict of interest shall declare that at the opening of the hearing on the matter and shall recuse himself or herself from all participation in hearing and deciding the case.

If an objection is raised to a member's participation in a case by a party to that case or by another board member and that member does not recuse himself or herself, the remaining members of the Board shall by majority vote rule on the objection.[16]

When a member is recused, that member shall absent himself or herself from the hearing room for the duration of the board's hearing, deliberation, and vote on that matter.[17]

E.    Board members shall not discuss any quasi-judicial case with, or receive any information about a case from, any parties to the case, other board members, or from other interested persons outside the

---

14. The law is uncertain as to whether a recused member may testify in a case. To avoid the appearance of undue influence on fellow board members, the practice is discouraged. Some rules prohibit it altogether.

15. These provisions on conflicts of interest are mandated by G.S. 160A-388(e)(2).

16. The provision on resolving objections to participation is mandated by G.S. 160A-388(e)(2).

17. An alternative to leaving the room would be a requirement that the recused board member sit in the audience rather than with the board during consideration of the matter.

evidentiary hearing on that case. No Board member shall conduct an investigation or gather facts about the case outside the evidentiary hearing. A Board member may visit the site of a pending case provided that visit is disclosed at the evidentiary hearing. Board members may seek and receive general information about ordinance and planning provisions pertaining to the case from the Chair, the town attorney, or town staff (except when a staff member is a party or an adversarial witness), provided any factual queries regarding the pending case itself shall only be made in open session at the evidentiary hearing.

F.    Board members shall not vote on the merits of any quasi-judicial matter unless the board member has either attended the evidentiary hearing on that matter or has thoroughly reviewed the full hearing record for that matter.[18]

G.    Board members shall not express individual opinions or judgments regarding a pending quasi-judicial case prior to the determination of that case.

V. MEETINGS.

A.    Regular Meetings. Regular meetings of the Board shall be held on the first Thursday of each month at ___ p.m. in the _____ Meeting Room of the _____ Building; provided that meetings may be held at any other convenient place, date or time in the Town if directed by the Chair in advance of the meeting and proper notice is given in accordance with applicable provisions of the Town Code and state law. The clerk to the Board shall make the schedule of regular meetings available to the public and shall post a copy of the schedule on the Town web site.

Regular meetings and hearings may be rescheduled by the Chair if a scheduled meeting or hearing cannot be held because of a holiday, weather, lack of a quorum, or other unusual circumstance. Notice of a rescheduled meeting shall be provided in the same means as required for a special meeting.

---

18. Alternatively, some rules (and some city charters) prohibit a board member from voting on a case unless the member has attended the evidentiary hearing on the matter.

When an evidentiary hearing will be conducted at a regular or special meeting, all required notices to the parties must be provided within the times set by state law and the UDO.

B.   Special Meetings. Special meetings of the Board may be called at any time by the Chair in accordance with Section _____ of the Town Code and applicable provisions of the Open Meetings Law, North Carolina General Statute 143-318.12. At least forty-eight (48) hours' written notice of the time and place of a special meeting shall be given by the clerk to the Board to each member of the Board and to each news organization and person requesting such notice. This notice may be provided by electronic mail. This notice shall also be posted on the Town web site.

Special meetings may be called by the Chair as necessary for Board training, work sessions, a heavy workload, or the conduct of Board business.

C.   Cancellation of Meetings. If there are no quasi-judicial cases to be heard or other business before the Board, if there is a weather emergency or similar situation, or if so many regular and alternate members indicate that they will not be able to attend that a quorum will not be available, the Chair may cancel a regular meeting by giving written and oral notice to all Board members. If feasible, notice of cancellation shall be made not less than twenty-four (24) hours before the time set for the meeting. The clerk to the Board shall post a notice of the meeting cancellation at the regular meeting location.

D.   Quorum. A quorum of the Board, necessary to meet, shall consist of three members of the Board, but the Board shall not vote on any questions related to an appeal of a decision or a determination of the Zoning Officer or an application for a variance or special use permit when fewer than four voting members of the Board are present. If fewer than five voting members of the Board are present, a party to a quasi-judicial matter may request that the hearing be continued until five voting members are present. Whenever during a meeting a quorum ceases to be present, if no objection is raised by a member of the Board, the Board may continue to hear evidence and debate but may not vote on any action except to adjourn.

E.   Hearing Deferrals and Continuances. Once a quasi-judicial case
     has been noticed for hearing, the Board generally expects the case
     to be heard at that time. An applicant may make a written request
     to delay consideration of a case to the next scheduled meeting,
     provided that the request is received at least twenty-four (24) hours
     prior to the scheduled meeting. Except for good cause shown, if an
     applicant fails to appear at a meeting to prosecute his or her appli-
     cation, and the hearing has been continued one (1) time before,
     the Board may dismiss the application for failure to prosecute. An
     application that has been dismissed may be resubmitted upon pay-
     ment of applicable fees.
         The Board may in its discretion continue any hearing when the
     Board deems that to be reasonable in order to receive additional
     evidence or to further deliberate. In all instances the Board shall
     decide cases within a reasonable time.

F.   Voting. All regular members shall vote on any issue unless they
     have disqualified themselves for one or more of the reasons stated
     in Section IV.[19] Alternate members shall vote on any issue for
     which they are seated in place of regular members unless they have
     disqualified themselves for one or more of the reasons stated in
     Section IV.
         The required vote to issue a variance shall be four-fifths of all
     members eligible to vote on the matter. If a motion to approve a
     variance does not receive the affirmative vote of four-fifths of those
     members eligible to vote, the variance shall be deemed denied.
     When this occurs, members who did not cast an affirmative vote
     on granting the variance shall state for the record their rationale
     for casting a negative vote. The required vote to decide any other
     quasi-judicial matter shall be a simple majority of all members
     eligible to vote on the matter.
         In all other matters the vote of a majority of the voting members
     present shall decide issues before the Board. The Chair votes as any
     other Board member.

---

19. Some rules include a provision similar to the statute applicable to elected
boards, that a member who is present and eligible to vote but who does vote on a
motion is deemed to have cast an affirmative vote.

G.  <u>Conduct of Meetings</u>. All meetings shall be open to the public, except for closed sessions as allowed by law. The order of business at regular meetings shall be as follows:

    i. Call to order, roll call, and announcements;

    ii. Action on minutes of previous meetings, including acceptance and correction;

    iii. Hearing, consideration, and determination of cases;

    iv. Reports of committees;

    v. Unfinished business;

    vi. New business;

    vii. Adjournment.

Without objection from a member, the Chair, or other member presiding at the meeting, may change the order of business, the order in which cases are heard, and rule on requests to withdraw or continue a case. Upon objection, the issue shall be put to a vote of the Board.

H.  <u>Agenda and Meeting Materials</u>. An agenda for each meeting and hearing shall be prepared by the clerk to the Board and shall be distributed to all members of the Board, applicants with cases to be heard, and any other interested person who has made a written request to receive an agenda. The agenda shall be distributed at least one week prior to regular meetings and two days prior to special meetings.

Written briefs, documents, letters, and staff reports may be submitted to Board members by the clerk to the Board prior to an evidentiary hearing, provided that any such material is also submitted to all parties to that case at the time they are submitted to Board members.[20] Staff may establish reasonable deadlines for submission of any such material to be distributed prior to the hearing. Such materials shall be distributed at the same time the meeting agenda is distributed. Any such material shall be part of the hearing record and introduced as documentary evidence at the evidentiary hearing. Board members shall endeavor to review the materials prior to the hearing.

---

20. Many boards prefer to receive written materials that will be introduced at the hearing in advance so as to allow review in preparation for the hearing. That is allowed but not mandated by these rules.

I.  Meeting Recordings. The Secretary shall make audio or video recordings of each meeting and hearing. Electronic recordings that may be used to generate transcripts for judicial review as needed shall be made of each meeting and shall be held for safekeeping by the Secretary in accordance with record retention policies set by state law and town ordinance. Any party to a quasi-judicial proceeding may request a verbatim transcript of the evidentiary hearing, with the cost of preparation of the transcript borne by the party making that request. Any person may make an audio or video recording of any Board hearing or meeting, provided it is done in a manner that does not disrupt the hearing or meeting.

J.  Oaths. All witnesses presenting testimony in evidentiary hearings shall be sworn in. Oaths may be administered by the Chair or the clerk to the Board. An affirmation may be made by any witness with a religious objection to swearing.

K.  Subpoenas. Persons with standing on a quasi-judicial matter before the Board may make a written request to subpoena for witnesses or to compel the production of evidence. The Chair shall issue subpoenas determined to be reasonable in nature and scope and not oppressive. The Chair shall rule on any objections or motions to quash subpoenas. The Chair's decisions on subpoenas may be appealed to the full Board.

## VI. APPEALS AND APPLICATIONS.

A.  Types of Appeals and Applications.

1. The Board shall hear and decide all appeals from final, binding written decisions or determinations made by the Zoning Administrator as provided by the UDO and by state statutes.

2. The Board shall hear and decide petitions for variances from the zoning ordinance and other such ordinances as provided by the UDO.

3. The Board shall hear and decide special or conditional use permits as assigned by the UDO.

4. The Board shall make interpretations of the Zoning Map, including disputed questions of zoning district boundary lines and similar questions that may arise from administration of the development regulations of the Town of _____.

5. The Board shall hear and decide appeals from decisions of the Historic Preservation Commission on certificates of appropriateness, provided that in such appeals the Board shall take no new evidence but shall review the decision in the nature of certiorari based on the record before the Historic Preservation Commission.[21]

6. The Board shall also hear and decide all matters referred to it or upon which it is required to pass by the UDO and any other matters assigned to it by ordinance or by law.

B. Procedure for Filing Appeals and Applications.

1. An appeal of a decision or determination of the Zoning Administrator shall be filed with the city clerk or such other officer as designated by the UDO. The notice of the appeal shall state the grounds for the appeal. No appeal shall be heard by the Board unless the appeal is filed within thirty (30) days of written or constructive notice of the order or determination made by the Zoning Administrator.[22]

2. Applications for variances and special use permits shall be accompanied by a site plan of sufficient size and accuracy to enable the Board to see the precise location and size of the variance and/or nature and location of the special use permit being sought. Such application shall specifically state the type of variance or special use permit sought. Upon submission of an application, the Zoning Administrator shall determine if these requirements are satisfied.

3. All appeals, applications, and any other matter coming before the Board shall be made upon the form for that purpose.

4. All required information required shall be complete and all required fees paid before an appeal, application, or other matter shall be considered as having been filed.

5. An applicant may withdraw any appeal, application, or other matter prior to the start of the evidentiary hearing on that matter. A withdrawal shall be made in writing. Upon with-

---

21. If the ordinance provides for appeals from any other decision in the local government's development regulations, they should be listed in this section.

22. These provisions are mandated by G.S. 160A-388(b1).

drawal the case is closed. A new application and fee must be submitted if the application is renewed.

C.   Evidentiary Hearings.

1. Time. After receipt of an appeal, application, or other matter, the clerk to the Board shall schedule the matter for hearing at the first available regular or special meeting scheduled within thirty (30) days from acceptance of a complete application.

2. Notice.[23] The Board shall give notice of evidentiary hearings on quasi-judicial cases by first-class mail to the person whose appeal or application is the subject of the hearing, to the owner of the affected property if the owner did not initiate the hearing, and to the owners of all parcels of land abutting the parcel of land that is the subject of the hearing. The notice shall be posted in the mail at least ten but not more than twenty-five days prior to the date of the hearing. A notice of the hearing shall also be prominently posted on the property that is the subject of the hearing (or the adjacent street right-of-way) in this same time period.

If a hearing is set for a given date and a quorum of the Board is not then present, the hearing shall be continued until the next regular Board meeting by announcement by the Chair without further advertisement. In addition, the Board may, without further advertisement, continue a hearing to a date certain after the hearing has been called to order.

The hearing notice shall include the location of the property subject to the hearing, the general nature of the matter being heard, and the date, time, and location of the hearing.

3. Conduct of Evidentiary Hearing. Any party may appear in person or by agent or by attorney at the hearing. The order of business for hearing shall be as follows:

a. The Chair, or such person as the Chair may direct, shall give an opening statement regarding the nature of the hearing and the process that will be followed. The Chair

---

23. This provision reflects the mailed and posted notice required by state law, N.C. G.S. 160A-388(a2). Notice published in a local newspaper is not required by state law but may be added if desired.

shall poll all Board members participating in the case as to any ex parte communications, bias, or conflicts of interest. Issues regarding standing, participation of board members in consideration of the case, or other jurisdictional issues shall be addressed. Witnesses to offer testimony may be sworn in.

b. The Chair or the staff shall provide a preliminary statement of the case, including a summary of the facts and relevant ordinance provisions. Staff shall present the application, supporting materials, staff report, and any other written materials received and distributed prior to the hearing for introduction into the hearing record.

c. The applicant shall present evidence and argument in support of the application or appeal taken.

d. Parties opposed to the application, including the staff from whom an appeal is being taken, may present evidence and argument.

e. Other persons may present relevant evidence.

f. Staff shall make a recommendation to the Board concerning requests for special use permits and variances.[24]

g. Parties may present rebuttal evidence.

h. Closing statements or summaries may be made by parties to the case and staff.

i. The Board shall deliberate on and make a determination of the case.

Witnesses may be called and factual evidence may be submitted. The Chair must recognize witnesses before they are heard and confirm that they are under oath. The Chair shall allow all witnesses to be heard but may limit testimony or evidence that is irrelevant, repetitive, incompetent, hearsay, or inadmissible opinion testimony. The Chair shall allow the parties to the case to make direct and cross-examination of witnesses and to present rebuttal evidence. The Chair may establish reasonable procedures to assure

24. An optional provision that may be deleted: Some boards prefer not to receive a recommendation from staff.

that is done in a fair, impartial, and efficient manner. Board members may ask questions of any witness.

The Board shall not be limited to consideration of such evidence as would be admissible in a court of law, but all decisions must be based on competent, material, and substantial evidence properly placed in the hearing record. Board members may view the premises before arriving at a decision, but any key facts observed by members shall be disclosed at the hearing and made part of the record.

Upon completion of the presentation of evidence and recommendation by the staff, Board members shall discuss the case among themselves in open session and may recall any witness to ask further questions and otherwise deliberate among themselves. Board members shall not discuss the case or give opinions on the evidence until initial presentation of the case is completed.

4. Rehearings. An application for a rehearing may be made to the Board and shall contain evidence that there has been a substantial change in the facts or conditions of the case. The Board may decide to conduct a full evidentiary hearing to consider such application. The application for rehearing shall be denied by the Board if, from the record, it finds there has been no substantial change in facts or conditions. If the Board finds that there has been a change, it shall thereupon treat the request in the same manner as a new application.

D. Decisions.

1. Time. Decisions by the Board shall be made in a reasonable time from the completion of the evidentiary hearing.[25] A decision may not be continued indefinitely.

2. Motion and Voting. Voting on an appeal, application, or other matter shall be in accordance with the provisions of the Town Code and the General Statutes. A vote on a request for a variance, special, or conditional use permit or on an appeal

---

25. Some rules set a specific deadline for making a decision, such as "A decision shall be made within 45 days of conclusion of the hearing unless the Board for good cause extends that time."

of a staff determination shall be in the form of a motion to approve the request, and such motions shall require a second.[26] A motion made to determine a quasi-judicial matter shall state specifically any conditions desired to be made a part of that decision and shall reference, if appropriate, any documents or maps submitted as a part of that application. Any such references made in the motion shall, if approved, be part of the record and decision in that case. The vote of each member shall be recorded. If a request or application is not approved, the members voting not to approve shall state for the record the factual findings and rationale that support their opposition.

3. <u>Form</u>. All decisions of the Board on quasi-judicial matters shall be reduced to writing as soon as practicable after the case is decided. The written decision shall reflect the Board's determination of contested facts and the application of the pertinent standards to those facts. The written decision shall be signed by the Chair or other duly authorized member of the Board.[27] After signature, the written decision shall be filed with the Clerk to the Board and delivered to the parties.

4. <u>Effective Date and Filing</u>. Decisions of the Board on quasi-judicial matters are effective upon filing the written decision with the Clerk to the Board and the delivery of the decision to the applicant, the property owner if that entity is not the applicant, and to any other person who filed a written request for a copy of the decision at the evidentiary hearing on the matter. The decision may be delivered by personal service, first-class mail, or electronic mail.[28]

5. <u>Public Records of Decisions</u>. The decisions of the Board shall be a public record available for inspection at all reasonable

---

26. Requiring motions to be made in the affirmative simplifies voting calculations—particularly determining whether a variance request is supported by four-fifths of the full Board or other cases are supported by a majority of the full Board.

27. These provisions are required by G.S. 160A-388(e2). Some rules require that written decision documents be presented to the full Board for approval, usually required to be done at the next regular meeting following the vote on the decision.

28. These provisions are required by G.S. 160A-388(e2).

times. All decisions shall be entered into the minutes of the Board. The Clerk to the Board shall maintain copies of all written decisions of the Board.

E.    Amendments.

These rules may be amended without prior notice by unanimous vote. Otherwise, consideration of the proposed amendment shall be set over to the next regular or special meeting.

## VII. ANNUAL REPORT TO PLANNING BOARD AND TOWN COUNCIL.

The Board, with the assistance of staff, shall prepare and submit to the Town Council a report of its activities for each fiscal year. The annual report shall contain a description of the Board (its membership, officers, attendance, and the number of meetings held) and a statement of the number of each type of case heard and a summary of the actions taken. The annual report also may include any other matters the Board deems appropriate for inclusion. The annual report shall be presented to the Town Council by September of each year.

# Subject Index

*Page numbers in italics are for illustrative materials.*

## O

oaths
> boards of adjustment, oath of office for, 14–15
> conscientious objection to, 15, 36
> sample rules of procedure on, *149*
> of witnesses, 16, 35–36, *36*, 39

officers of boards of adjustment, 16, *139–41. See also* chair of board of adjustment

open meetings, 17–18, 21, 45–46

ordinances, use of in making a decision
> avoiding absurd or bizarre interpretations, 103
> general rules of interpretation, 102–103
> purpose and intent of, 73, 74, 102

*Overton v. Camden County* (2002), 53n18

## P

parties with standing
> to appeal staff decisions, 98
> attorneys of, 28–29, 41
> in chair's script for meetings and evidentiary hearings, *132–33, 136*
> in evidentiary hearings, 28–32
> for judicial review, 107
> special damages and, 31–32, 107

"peculiar to the property" requirement for variances, 71–72

petition for judicial review, 105–6

plain meaning of ordinance, 101

planning boards, special use permit decisions assigned to, 79, 80

precedent, 58

pre-evidentiary hearing procedures, 5, 17–24

preliminary record, 20–21

*Premier Plastic Surgery Center, PLLC v. Board of Adjustment for Town of Matthews* (2011), 73n11

*Pritchard v. Elizabeth City* (1986), 101n11

private property and site visits, 21–22

property values
> special use permits, no significant adverse impacts of, 81, 83–84
> standing as party and, 31–32

proposed findings of fact and conclusions of law, 60

proximity and standing as party, 31–32

public health and safety. *See* safety issues

public meetings and public record requirements, 17–18, 21, 45–46, *154–55*

www.ingramcontent.com/pod-product-compliance
Lightning Source LLC
Chambersburg PA
CBHW050805270326
41926CB00025B/4548